CHRIST AND THE MEDIA

by

Malcolm Muggeridge

WILLIAM B. EERDMANS PUBLISHING COMPANY

Also in this series of
London Lectures in Contemporary Christianity

CHRISTIANS AND MARXISTS
by José Miguez Bonino

ISSUES OF LIFE AND DEATH
by Norman Anderson

Reprinted, August 1978

Library of Congress Cataloging in Publication Data

Muggeridge, Malcolm, 1903-
    Christ and the media.

    1.   Mass media — Moral and religious aspects.   I.   Title.
P94.M8   1978   261.8'3   77-15575
ISBN 0-8028-3508-2

PREFACE

THE INFLUENCE OF the mass media upon us all is continuous, insistent and pervasive; and no modern medium is more powerful than television. It would be impossible to make any assessment of contemporary society without taking it into account. Recent studies reveal that in Britain the average adult watches television for sixteen to eighteen hours a week, which represents about eight years of the human life span or one-seventh of the time we are awake. Is this electronic input beneficial, harmful or neutral, or all three at different times and in different ways? In particular, can there be a distinctively Christian viewpoint on such a question? In what sense is it proper to bracket 'Christ' and 'the media'?

These are some of the questions which were in our minds when choosing the media as the topic for the 1976 London Lectures in Contemporary Christianity and inviting Malcolm Muggeridge to be the lecturer. For the purpose of this annual lectureship, sponsored by the Langham Trust, is to promote Christian thinking about important contemporary issues.

Throughout his life Malcolm Muggeridge has been a gifted communicator. With words and images, as lecturer, journalist and author, on radio and television, he has fascinated, delighted, provoked — and sometimes infuriated — his audiences. Moreover, the publication of *Jesus Rediscovered* in 1969 told the world of his personal commitment to Jesus Christ, while in *Jesus, the*

Man who Lives (1975) his Christian faith is seen to burn more brightly still. So several hundreds of people came to the three lectures, which were given in All Souls Church, Langham Place, in November 1976, and took part in the question-time which followed.

Malcolm Muggeridge has now revised his lectures for publication. The questions and answers, together with the chairmen's short speeches, are also included in this volume as appendices; they have been sub-edited, but without in any way altering their substance and style. Since the reader will find there the remarks I made at the end of the three lectures, I will add no further comment here, except to say that, instead of accepting any royalties from this book, Malcolm Muggeridge has with characteristic generosity assigned them to the Evangelical Literature Trust which finances pastors' book clubs and other literary projects in the Third World.

JOHN STOTT

Chairman, London Lectures in Contemporary Christianity

FOREWORD

DURING MY VISIT to London in 1954 a famous journalist by the name of Malcolm Muggeridge interviewed me over the British Broadcasting Corporation television. I did not know at the time that it was his first television interview, and that in time he would become one of Britain's best known television personalities. He was known for his brilliant mind and clever manner. He was also known as something of a cynic about most things, including religion and (especially) visiting American evangelists.

Little did I realize that almost exactly twenty years later it would be my privilege to introduce Malcolm Muggeridge as my dear friend and fellow Christian to over three thousand Christian leaders from around the world at the Lausanne International Congress on World Evangelization. The story of his spiritual pilgrimage from unbelief to faith in Christ is thrilling, and today Malcolm Muggeridge is a bold and perceptive spokesman for the Kingdom of God.

The Langham Trust, under the leadership of my good friend John Stott, has done a great service to present for publication the 1976 London Lectures in Contemporary Christianity featuring Malcolm Muggeridge. They form an important contribution to the debate over the place of the media in today's society. They also are a challenging statement to Christians concerning our attitudes toward the media.

Few people in the entire world are better equipped than Malcolm Muggeridge to analyze and dissect the influence of the media from a Christian standpoint.

Muggeridge is always stimulating, and this series of lectures is no exception. The remarks of Sir Charles Curran, Sir Brian Young and Dr. John Stott are full of satire, humor and rebuttal, and include some thought-provoking points.

Much could be said about the numerous points Malcolm Muggeridge raises, but I would like to comment especially on two of them.

First, the basic theme of these lectures is Muggeridge's conviction that the media (particularly television) has had an extremely negative effect on our civilization, and that this effect can only be expected to grow. In other words, he sees television not as something neutral which can be used for good or ill. Instead he sees it always tending toward evil, not good. The technical complexities, necessity of editing, and the demands of the public make the television producer turn reality into fantasy.

Is he right? Is television beyond redemption? Whether or not he is right, he will make us think.

It is at this point Muggeridge especially presents a challenge to Christians. He admits that the Christian may work within the media, although he has few guidelines for this. He also admits there are times when television can be used to convey Christian truth, although he sees this as a rarity.

He is considerably more skeptical about Christians using television than I personally would be. Perhaps this is because of the differences between British and American television. I have been very grateful for the opportunities I have had personally over British television (whether in interviews, addresses, or crusade coverage) to share the Gospel of Christ. At the same time, it may be true that British television does not generally give time to anything which is evangelical in content. In American television, on the other hand, virtually any religious group can purchase television time for programming. I know there is some question about how long this will continue. However, I am personally thankful for every opportunity we have for presenting the Gospel by means of the mass media, especially television. There are many thousands of people whose lives have been changed by seeing a television program which presented the Gospel. Many of these people would almost certainly never have gone to a church or attended an evangelistic crusade. I often think of Paul's words in I Corinthians 9:22-23: "I have become all things to all men so that by all possible means I might save some. I do all this for the sake of the gospel" (New International Version).

There is, I think, another issue which is very important, although it is not Mr. Muggeridge's main point. Although he stresses the role of the media, he also reminds us constantly of the nature of the world in which we live, which has been affected so deeply and tragically by sin. He reminds us with unforgettable eloquence of the way all the world's values are opposed to the values of the Kingdom of God. He reminds us with penetrating insight of the folly of worldly power, fortune, and success. He reminds us with majestic simplicity of the ultimate overthrow of all human systems of thought and action, and of the certain triumph of the Kingdom of God. He challenges us to live for Christ in the midst of a dying world, doing all we can to help people glimpse the eternal reality and glory of Christ's Kingdom.

In a sense the problem of the media is but a symptom of a deeper problem — the problem of the human heart, alienated from God. Only the radical transformation Christ brings will ever be able to solve this fundamental problem. Malcolm Muggeridge has seen this clearly, and I am thankful that he reminds us once again of the only hope for the human race — Jesus Christ, our Lord.

BILLY GRAHAM

CONTENTS

Introduction   11
Lecture One: The Fourth Temptation   23
Lecture Two: The Dead Sea Video Tapes   43
Lecture Three: Through the Eye   60
Questions following the first lecture   81
Questions following the second lecture   89
Questions following the third lecture   98
Chairman's Speech:
                 Sir Charles Curran   111
                 Sir Brian Young   117
                 The Rev. John Stott   121

But his word was in mine heart as a burning fire shut up in my bones, and I was weary with forbearing.

Jeremiah

INTRODUCTION

THE ONLY CREDENTIALS I can justly claim in holding forth
about the media is that I am a veteran operator. For almost the
whole of my working life — since 1930, in fact — I have been
in this business in one capacity or another, with pen and voice
and face. Even when I joined the army as a private in 1939, I
soon found myself an Intelligence officer and, as such, to all
intents and purposes, back with the media. Though I cannot
pretend not to have on the whole enjoyed this fraudulent
occupation, if only because it meets certain requirements of a
restless disposition, besides catering for a *voyeur* attitude
towards those set in authority over us and their doings, I have
never been able to take it quite seriously. There is a built-in
element of farce which keeps it teetering on the brink of
absurdity.

As I make this point, scenes from the past crowd in on me.
For instance, following Harold Macmillan, when he was Prime
Minister, round a collective farm in the Ukraine, he attired in
his best plus-fours, and, when the time came for him to deliver
a speech, pointing out that in the eleventh century a Ukrainian
princess had married into the British royal family, thereby
putting Anglo-Ukrainian relations on a sound and cordial basis.
Or trailing along behind President Truman when he was taken,
very early in the morning after a festive evening of American-
Canadian conviviality, to see the Niagara Falls, the vehicle

provided for him being the local hearse. Or again, accompanying the Emperor of Japan on his first visit to Hiroshima after its atomic bombardment, he wearing a neat suit and trilby hat, a get-up considered appropriate now that, in accordance with General MacArthur's directive, he was no longer a Sun God but just a democratic sovereign, and supporting this rôle by raising his hat at regular intervals, quite irrespective of whether or not there was any acclamation to respond to. Or, yet again, running into Earl Attlee in the cavernous Reform Club one evening, he on his way to some official function, in tails and a white waistcoat, and so laden with metal attached to his tiny person in the way of decorations of one sort and another that I marvelled he did not collapse under its weight.

Such episodes — and happily their number is legion — represent a special blessing whereby workers in the media are spared total immersion in them, whether, like the American Knights of Watergate, to accept their pretentions utterly, or just to collapse on to a psychiatrist's couch. My own attitude has always been decidedly ambivalent; on the one hand, I have seized every opportunity to hold the media up to ridicule and contempt; on the other, I have continued to be a practitioner, with, I suppose I may say, some measure of professional competence, if not success. This has proved baffling to well-wishers, and to ill-wishers a ready opening to be abusive. At different times I have produced various justifications for going on doing what I purport to despise. For instance, that, as a television performer, I see myself as a man playing a piano in a brothel, who includes 'Abide With Me' in his repertoire in the hope of thereby edifying both clients and inmates. Re-reading recently Boswell's *Life of Johnson*, I came across the following exchange, which I adopted on the spot as perfectly exemplifying my present attitude to television:

GOLDSMITH: I think, Dr. Johnson, you don't go to the theatre now. You give yourself no more concern about a new play than if you had never had anything to do with the stage.

JOHNSON: Why, Sir, our tastes greatly alter. The lad does not care for a child's rattle, and the old man does not care for the young man's whore.

GOLDSMITH: Nay, Sir, but your muse was not a whore.

JOHNSON: Sir, I do not think she was. But as we advance in the journey of life, we drop some of the things that have pleased us; whether it be that we are fatigued and don't choose to carry so many things any further, or that we find other things we like better.

The precise motives which induce human beings to engage in this activity rather than that, to seek a diocese rather than a constituency, an editorial chair rather than a pulpit or a soapbox, are usually complicated and difficult to unravel with honesty. In my case, in my various avocations, drift has played a large part; someone has made a proposal about something or other, and I have accepted it without any serious consideration, forgetful of what I have undertaken until an air-ticket arrives, or a summons to some function or other at which, I am horrified to note, I am expected to be an active participant. This was precisely how television came into my life. It happened some twenty years ago when I was editor of *Punch*, and the particular assignment I accepted in this easy-going way was — some would say signficantly — to provide a commentary for a film of Billy Graham's Harringay Crusade, and afterwards to interview Billy himself in front of the cameras. It all passed off smoothly enough, and thenceforth I found myself participating fairly regularly in the BBC's first TV magazine programme, *Panorama*.

These were the early days of television, and it never occurred to me then that there was any intrinsic difference between television journalism and any other variety, written or spoken. Later, as I became involved in the obsessive interest television has come to arouse, I participated in the interminable inquest as to whether it can be considered a debit or credit item in our popular culture:

as stimulating, or merely reflecting, the growing depravity and violence of our way of life; as a cause or a consequence of growing illiteracy; as a window on the world, or a mirror reflecting all too faithfully our world's absurdities and inanities. My precise motives for continuing none the less to do my stint before the cameras were mixed: cupidity played a part, in the sense that talking seemed an easier way of earning money than writing, though in terms of mental wear-and-tear this is probably a fallacy; as did also vanity, in the sense that there is liable to be a certain infantile satisfaction in being recognised, though this, too, can be distressing and disturbing; also vainglory, in the sense that to be what is called a television personality is liable to get delusions of grandeur, as well as, again, the converse — a sense of shame. What I can say with truth is that I have never once walked off a set after a programme without feeling a strange sort of desolation, and that making off from Lime Grove or the Television Centre, even the streets of Shepherd's Bush have seemed like paradise.

Despite these dubieties, in the ordinary way, I suppose, I should just have drifted on, doing commentaries for documentaries, appearing in talk shows of one sort and another, acting as anchorman as and when required, interviewing the relatively few personages considered to have interview potential (I could name up to a hundred in this category, most of them, like an old pack of cards, showing signs of having been much passed from hand to hand by the studio maestros), and in the fulness of time making my final bow, perhaps considered by that time to be a lesser Dimbleby, and so rating a momentary blacking out of TV screens to signalise my definitive departure to another place, where, as I devoutly hope, there is neither filming nor the showing of films.

That things did not happen so was due rather to certain changes in myself than to outside circumstances. I came to detect, as it were, a golden thread of reality running through the fantasy of happenings and news about them, of the ego and its appetites, of power and its creatures — the great ones of the earth, victims of that most dangerous of all poisons, from Caesar's laurel crown. Following this golden thread, I was led hesitantly, with many stumblings and meanderings, to the realisation that the Kingdom not of this world proclaimed in the New Testament is, in fact, our true habitat, and that those other kingdoms of the earth which the Devil has on offer bear the same relation to Christ's Kingdom as the travel brochures do to all the delectable places they try to persude us to visit. In the light of this discovery, the media came to seem the wrong way round: their light was darkness, their facts were fancy, their documentation was myth. Across his copy of Bacon's Essays, one of the early scriptures of the age of science, Blake scrawled: 'Good news for Satan's Kingdom!' I found myself wanting to scrawl the same words across the offerings of the various TV channels, especially the more serious ones. The media have, indeed, provided the Devil with perhaps the greatest opportunity accorded him since Adam and Eve were turned out of the Garden of Eden. I only wish C. S. Lewis had lived long enough to deal with this in another masterly *Screwtape Letter*, pointing out the advantages of infiltrating the media, on the production or performing side (better, probably, the former), where a few deft touches could undermine the faith of a lifetime, and impeccable humanistic sentiments open the way to debauching a human soul on a scale that the Prince of Darkness himself might envy. Indeed, one imagines Old Nick disconsolately shaking his head over how the young devils nowadays have it made: all they need to do is just to get into religious broadcasting, and what chances present themselves! Screwtape had it drummed into him that, in devilish terms, there is far more mileage in good humane people like Eleanor Roosevelt than in wicked cruel ones like Stalin. King Herod has always had a bad press for slaughtering the innocents, but let Screwtape keep it in mind that nowadays a good campaign on the media for legalised abortion will facilitate the slaughter of millions on the highest humanitarian principles before they are even born.

There is a very funny book to be written about becoming a Christian in the last decades of the twentieth century. The comedy lies in the fact that, to most contemporary minds, there must be some extraneous explanation of such an out-of-the-way reversal of attitudes other than the intrinsic truth and irresistible appeal of the Christian faith as revealed in the birth, ministry, death and resurrection of its founder. So the most bizarre theories are propounded to account for something that has been happening continuously, and affecting all sorts and conditions of people, for some twenty centuries past. P. G. Wodehouse was fond of recalling how a fellow novelist of enormous solemnity — Hugh Walpole — was heard to remark, when it came to his notice that Hilaire Belloc had pronounced Wodehouse to be the most accomplished writer of his time: 'Now, whatever can Belloc have meant by that?' In the same sort of way, one's friends ask what can possibly account for so weird, not to say outrageous a decision, publicly announced, as to opt for Christ rather than for Marx, or D. H. Lawrence, or Jung, or one of the contemporary gurus like the Maharishi who seem to be constantly moving Westwards these days.

In my case, old friends have a ready explanation to hand in my evident senility: the poor fellow, they say, shaking their heads sadly, used to be quite amusing until this unaccountable aberration seized him, since when, it must be admitted, he has been an unconscionable bore. The manner in which they none the less very decently go on being friendly and considerate suggests how they might have been expected to behave — though in that case they would have been more genuinely sympathetic — if one had been arrested in the park for what used in more reticent days to be called 'a serious offence' and they were being very nice about it. The others — not so amicably inclined — look for some more sinister explanation, expatiating upon how old lechers when they become impotent

are notoriously liable to denounce lechery, seeking to deprive
others of pleasures no longer within their reach; how a clown
whose act has staled will look around for some gimmick, however grotesque and unconvincing, to draw attention to himself.
As for the clergy — whereas they were disposed to look kindly
on someone billed by the media as a poor man's Voltaire, his
reappearance on the screen as a poor man's St. Augustine is
little to their taste. For me, the tone was set when, having
resigned as Rector of Edinburgh Univeristy rather than sponsor
a demand by the students for a free handout of contraceptives
by the university medical unit, the first salvo in the counter-
attack was delivered by none other than the University's Roman
Catholic chaplain. It reminded me at the time of how, when
Don Quixote brought about the release of a chain of galley
slaves, the first thing they did when they were freed was to pelt
him with stones. Many other such farcical adventures befell me
in and out of the studios in trying to convey through the
instrumentality of the media, especially television, something
of the illumination I had experienced, for which, however,
thanks are due. God savours even his routine orders of the day
with irony. How understandable is that resigned 'Here am I'
with which the prophets in the Old Testament answer his
summons; and when the disciples have responded to our Lord's
call to leave everything and follow him, it is made clear to them
they are still not to be let off fishing, though now, they are told
— I am sure with a chuckle — they will have to bait their
hooks and set their nets to catch men, not fish.

It was in the light of my experiences, some puzzling, some
hilarious and some rather agonising, in what passes for being
religious broadcasting, that I responded eagerly to John Stott's
invitation to speak about Christ and the media. In practice I
found it much more difficult than I had anticipated; indeed, I
am conscious of having failed to produce other than an im-
pressionistic, idiosyncratic survey of a subject that requires
more scholarship than I possess and more diligent concentration

of purpose than my journalistic habits of thought and exposition have provided.

As our country in particular, and the Western world altogether, moves further and further away from the Christian assumptions on which our way of life has hitherto been, at any rate ostensibly, based, the difficulties of those responsible for the conduct of the media will grow ever more acute, unless, as seems to be probable, if not certain, they relapse into acceptance of whatever comes along, contenting themselves with, at most, delaying our seemingly inexorable descent into moral vacuity. The first Director-General of the BBC, John Reith, had no doubts whatsoever that it was his duty, not just to put out specifically Christian programmes, but to ensure that Christianity provided the ethical and spiritual terms of reference for the Corporation's whole output. Another Director-General, Sir William Haley, could say in 1948: 'We are citizens of a Christian country, and the BBC — an institution set up by the State — bases its policy upon a positive attitude towards the Christian values. It seeks to safeguard those values and to foster acceptance of them. The whole preponderant weight of its programmes is directed to this end.' Sir William Haley's successors have steadily retreated from this position, on the way throwing up a smokescreen of talk about justice, freedom, tolerance, compassion, and an artist's right to refuse to be harnessed to current *mores* in fulfilling his duty to indict the present and proclaim the future. If I might be permitted to quote from the Broadcasting Section of the Longford Report on Pornography for which I was responsible:

It is behind this portentous smokescreen that BBC producers have been able with impunity to mount their increasingly 'outspoken' — which usually in practice means erotic — shows and plays, and explore and exploit the no-man's land of fantasy lying between drama and documentary. The pursuit of excellence recommended by Huw Weldon becomes the pursuit of notoriety, and copy which the popular Sunday newspapers might hesitate to run gets by as being the precious yield of unimpeded creativity.

I should like in conclusion to express my grateful thanks to Sir Charles Curran and Sir Brian Young for agreeing to preside over the first two lectures. In Sir Charles's case especially, it was a gesture of magnanimity. It was also most courteous of Sir Michael Swann, the Chairman of the Governors of the BBC and Vice-Chancellor of Edinburgh University when I was Rector, to attend the second lecture. The third lecture, at my special request, was presided over by John Stott. What he said on that occasion, though undeserved, will always be for me a precious memory. For the three chairmen's speeches, and Sir Michael Swann's remarks, see pp. 94-123.

LECTURES

THE FOURTH TEMPTATION

IT IS A truism to say that the media in general, and TV in particular, and BBC television especially, are incomparably the greatest single influence in our society today, exerted at all social, economic and cultural levels. This influence, I should add, is, in my opinion, largely exerted irresponsibly, arbitrarily, and without reference to any moral or intellectual, still less spiritual, guidelines whatsoever. Furthermore, if it is the case, as I believe, that what we still call Western civilisation is fast disintegrating, then the media are playing a major rôle in the process by carrying out, albeit for the most part unconsciously, a mighty brainwashing operation, whereby all traditional standards and values are being denigrated to the point of disappearing, leaving a moral vacuum in which the very concepts of Good and Evil have ceased to have any validity. Like a building site, which has been cleared, but with nothing erected on it; just a great, empty space, where rubbish is thrown, where children play and quarrel and fight, and layabouts sleep, and the rain collects in puddles. Future historians will surely see us as having created in the media a Frankenstein monster which no one knows how to control or direct, and marvel that we should have so meekly subjected ourselves to its destructive and often malign influence. More particularly as, in the case of the BBC, it is financed out of the public purse. Nor do I see within the various broadcasting agencies any force, actual or potential, capable of delivering us from being totally submerged in the world of fantasy the channels they control project.

I was reading recently the splendid words of the prophet Isaiah, quoted by the Apostle Paul when he first met the Roman Christians. Words, St. Paul explains, delivered to Isaiah by the Holy Ghost to be passed on to the recalcitrant children of Israel:

Hearing, ye shall hear and shall not understand, and seeing, ye shall see, and not perceive, for the heart of these people is waxed gross and their ears are dull of hearing and their eyes have they closed, lest they should see with their eyes, and hear with their ears, and understand with their hearts.

Paul went on to point to the Christian revelation as being the only means of making eyes truly see, and ears truly hear; of, as it were, bringing into sinc the crazy world of Nero's Rome. By the same token, I am more convinced than of anything else that I have ever thought, or considered, or believed, that the only antidote to the media's world of fantasy is the reality of Christ's Kingdom proclaimed in the New Testament. This is why I am particularly glad to have been asked to deliver these lectures by John Stott, for whom I have so great a regard and affection, and to deliver them here, in this church, where his and his successor's ministries have been so outstandingly effective, and which has now been so excellently reconstructed by their congregation's own efforts, rather than in some secular hall or lecture theatre, as was at one time considered.

At this point, perhaps because of the proximity of Broadcasting House, there looms up irresistibly before me the massive figure of John Reith. How at first sight bizarre it is, that he, a ferocious moralist and cradle Calvinist, should have been the founding father of the BBC as we know it today, convinced to the end of his life that if only he had remained in charge, the ship he had launched would never have come to fly the skull and crossbones, never have taken to piracy on the high seas!

One of the numerous pleasures of old age is the realisation that everything has to be just as it is, making what Blake called a 'Fearful Symmetry', whose meaning is transparently clear if only one has the code book and knows how to use it — the code book being, of course, the Gospels and Epistles and other related literature. Every happening, great and small, that is to say, is a parable whereby God speaks to us; and the art of life is to get the message. In the same sort of way, listening to great music, or reading great literature, or standing before great buildings, an inner rhythm is detected, and the heart rejoices, and a light breaks, which is none other than God's love shining through all his creation. 'How delightful,' Jean-Pierre de Caussade writes, 'the peace we enjoy when we have learned by faith to see God in this way through all creatures as through a transparent veil. Darkness becomes light and bitterness sweet.' Thus, when I had the job of attempting a tele-anatomy of Reith not long before he died, I came to realise that in some weird way he *was* the perfectly appropriate first compère or anchorman for the great media harlequinade; groaning and suffering, as he did, while the show was being got on the road, and then cursing it heartily for its subsequent ribald performances.

As it happens, I saw him on his death-bed, when a marvellous peace at last descended on that troubled spirit. At the same time, I found myself remembering the words he'd had inscribed at the entrance to Broadcasting House, and even seemed to hear him pronouncing them with great unction and emphasis:

This temple of the arts and muses is dedicated to Almighty God by the first governors of broadcasting in the year 1931, Sir John Reith being Governor General. It is their prayer that good seeds sown may bring forth a good harvest, that all things hostile to peace or purity may be banished from this house, that the people, inclining their ears to whatsoever things are beautiful, honest and of good report, may tread the paths of wisdom and righteousness.

How fortunate that the words are in Latin, not in English! Otherwise, for decency's sake, they would have had to be removed, or, like the seven commandments in Orwell's *Animal Farm*, adjusted.

Though the media as we know them today are a comparatively recent growth, a great deal, one way or another, has been written about them, and there are already — always a very ominous sign — in some of our more recently planted groves of academe, departments which specialise in the subject, with their due complement of professors, lecturers and other academic grades, all busily producing a plethora of theses on media subjects. Across the Atlantic, I need scarcely add, this development is even more marked than here. Not just the media themselves, but the study of the media, is very much a labour-intensive and growth industry. I have had occasion to read, or at any rate to review (which is by no means the same thing) quite a lot of this literature. In honesty, however, I must warn in advance any who may embark upon exploring it, that books about the media almost all have one, on the face of it, surprising feature in common — though their subject is communication, they display a singular incapacity to communicate themselves. Perhaps on consideration this is not so surprising as it may appear. In our strange world, it is the impotent who are prone to instruct us in the excellencies of potency, the dyspeptic who proclaim a dietary way to health and happiness, the opponents of capital punishment and killing seals who insist on the killing of unborn babies, and the much-married who turn to marriage counselling. So why not communicators who cannot communicate?

Here, by way of example, let me quote from the writings of a celebrated authority in this field, Marshall McLuhan, originator of the most famous of all media aphorisms, 'The medium is the message'. The following sentences are taken at random from his book *From Cliché to Archetype*.

Writing as a means of retrieving 'ancientry' led to a vast scrap heap of retrieved data even before the advent of 'lumpend paper'. The middenhide grows mountainous with the castoffs of cultures and technologies. One theme in 'middenhide' is the popular invisible quality of the environments created by new clichés or techniques. The forms of these technologies are imprinted not only on human language but on the outer world as well: 'But the world, mind, is, was and will be writing its own wrunes for ever, man, on all matters' gave us the 'ruins', the deciphering and retrieval of which fascinates the literate humanist.

What it does to the illiterate humanist, one can only imagine, but I know what it does to me — I can't make head or tail of it.

Among the writings on the media, too, there are inevitably numerous studies, as they are called, relating to particular aspects of TV like violence and eroticism. Ten thousand blameless housewives in Minnesota will be asked whether their tranquillity has been disturbed, their erotic impulses stimulated, and their nights disrupted by scenes of violence and debauchery on the television screen. The result is then punctiliously monitored, fed into a computer, tabulated and analysed. I personally am very sceptical about such investigations which, for instance, tend to support the contention that violence and eroticism on the television screen do not to any appreciable extent stimulate violent and erotic impulses off it. In this connection, I remember reading in *The New Statesman* about an experiment which, it was claimed, 'proved conclusively' that pornography does not have a corrupting effect. It seems that a Doctor C. Elthammer of the Stockholm Child Psychiatric Department arranged for some children between the ages of eleven and eighteen to see a film of a woman being raped by a group of intoxicated louts, then forced to have intercourse with a dog. None of the children, Doctor Elthammer triumphantly reported, were frightened during or after the film, but a proportion of the older girls did admit to being shocked, while two adults, also present, needed psychiatric treatment for a month afterwards. One idly wonders what, if anything, happened to the dog. I find it fascinating that credulity about scientifically stated absurdities should thus exceed the wildest examples of religious superstition. I have often thought it would be a very good idea to bring an African witch-doctor or medicine-man to London, and let him have an intensive course of looking at television advertisements. The good man, I fancy, would be green with envy as he recalled all the weary slogging he had done carrying his love-potions and ju-jus from African village to African village, when here in the West, with ostensibly the most civilised, the best educated and certainly the richest population in the world, there was this fathomless reservoir of credulity for all who cared to avail themselves of it.

Anyway, it would seem clear to me that, if edifying scenes on television uplift the viewers, it must also be true that un-edifying scenes degrade them. Furthermore, when very large sums of money are paid for advertising at peak viewing periods, as they are, it can only be because the often quite riduculously unconvincing advertisements shown in such expensively-purchased time do have sufficient drawing power to justify the expenditure. Every performer knows that television appearances have an impact, for good or ill. How can it possibly be doubted, then, that spectacles of carnality and violence likewise affect the viewer? As far as I am concerned, there are no studies that could be mounted capable of convincing me that the eight years of a normal life-span that an average Western man spends looking at the television screen have no appreciable influence on his *mores* or way of evaluating his existence. Happily, however, there is no occasion for me now to try and unravel the un-ravellable utterances of media experts like McLuhan — some-one, incidentally, whom I have met and liked, and shouldn't wish to seem to disparage, just because his writing sometimes reads to me like gibberish. Nor need I attempt to fathom the unfathomable studies. In these lectures I am concerned, not so much with the media as such, a subject of immense and indeterminate range, but with the degree to which, if at all, the reality of Christ, and of the words he spoke, and the Way he signposted and took himself, can be injected into the fantasy of the media and expounded in the context of their offerings. This is my subject.

'All the world's a stage,' Shakespeare said, but now it is the other way round. All the stage is a world, presented on a television screen, purporting to traffic in news, and convey real life in living colour (whatever that may mean), but in practice transporting the viewer into a Caliban's Island,

> full of noises,
> Sounds and sweet airs, that give delight,
> and hurt not,
> Sometimes a thousand twanging instruments
> Will hum about mine ears; and sometime
> voices
> That, if I then had wak'd after long sleep,
> Will make me sleep again; and then, in dreaming,
> The clouds methought would open and show riches
> Ready to drop upon me; that, when I wak'd,
> I cried to sleep again.

Thus the viewer, except that he never does wake, and so has no occasion to cry to sleep again. Only, occasionally, vague musings assail him. Is the blood real, or just ketchup? Were the shots actually fired, or just sound effects? Is it studio laughter, or people veritably laughing? Who can tell? The first time that ever I went out on a colour television filming expedition, I noticed that a member of the camera crew was carrying something rolled up under his arm. When I asked him what it was, he told me it was the plastic grass, real grass not being green enough for living colour. 'Keep the witch-hazel handy,' a floor

manager was instructed during the filming of a Nixon commercial during the 1972 Presidential election, 'we can't do the
sincerity bit if he's sweating.' *Cinema verité* or *cinema falsite*?
Not only *can* the camera lie, it always lies. To adapt a famous
saying of C. P. Scott, owner/editor of the *Manchester Guardian*
in the days of its greatness: 'Comment is free, but footage is
sacred.'

The prevailing impression I have come to have of the
contemporary scene is of an ever-widening chasm between the
fantasy in terms of which the media induce us to live, and the
reality of our existence as made in the image of God, as
sojourners in time whose true habitat is eternity. The fantasy is
all-encompassing; awareness of reality requires the seeing eye
which comes to those born again in Christ. It is like coming to
after an anaesthetic; the mists lift, consciousness returns, everything in the world is more beautiful than ever it was, because
related to a reality beyond the world — every thought clearer,
love deeper, joy more abounding, hope more certain. Who
could hesitate, confronted with this choice between an old
fantasy and a newly discovered reality? As well prefer the
coloured pictures of golden beaches and azure skies in the
travel supplements to the sea and the sky; mere erotic excitement to the ecstasy of love, life inside a camera to life inside a
universe as an infinitesimal participant in its Creator's purposes.
The choice is clear enough, but how can it best be presented?
With or without the media? Seeking their help or in despite of
them? Would St. Paul, when he was in Corinth, have agreed
to deliver an address during an interval in the games, which
were so like television today, being essentially purveyors of
spectator violence and spectator eroticism? Supposing there had
been a fourth temptation when our Lord encountered the Devil
in the wilderness — this time an offer of networked TV
appearances, in prime time, to proclaim and expound his
Gospel. Would this offer, too, have been rejected like the
others? If so, why?

Before attempting to answer these questions, let me try and establish my own credentials as a media man or, in St. Augustine's apt expression, 'a vendor of words', in the process, as I hope, providing a sort of tabloid conspectus of the media as they have existed and functioned in my time. I look back now on more than half a century of knock-about journalism of one sort or another, comprising pretty well everything in the business, from editorial pontificating to skittish gossip paragraphs, from datelined despatches from our special correspondent here, there and everywhere, to features on strange pets, or on living to be a hundred and forty in Georgia by eating yoghurt. Not to mention the strange interlude when, as editor of *Punch*, I undertook the sombre task of trying to make the English laugh. Then, with the coming of television, venturing into studios, where, seated under the arc-lights, and with the cameras' blood-shot eyes bearing down on me, the clapper-board clapped, the floor manager cried 'Action!', and off we went. 'Bishop, is there an afterlife?' when he'd been expecting something easy, like: 'Why are church congregations dwindling?' Poor Bishop Pike, say, late lamented, taking my arm on our way to the hospitality room and remarking: 'St. Paul, you know, was wrong about sex.' So we proceed, from 'Action!' to 'Cut!' On my death-bed, shall I hear a fateful voice from on high pronouncing that single word: 'Cut!'? I often fancy so.

Then out on location, that strange procession, hand-holding cameraman umbilically linked to sound recordist similarly laden, bearing before him, upheld like a phallus, a great gun-mike; behind them, producer and continuity girl pacing in unison, she with a large stopwatch dangling from her sweet neck, as it might be a lady mayoress's insignia; the whole cortège treading as delicately as caparisoned horses at a bullfight. Or a Vox Pop effort, one, in Chicago, never-to-be-forgotten, outside the *Tribune* Building in Michigan Avenue. Presenting a microphone — 'Excuse me, madam ... Beg pardon, sir ... In England, a new Prime Minister ... Harold Wilson ... Any comment?' No, none; clearly, along Michigan Avenue, Harold Wilson was not a name to conjure with. An extra poignancy was added to this total indifference to news of our brave new Premier making his bow upon the world's stage when I noticed, high above the *Tribune* Building, letters of fire spelling out every three minutes the legend: IN UK HOME OUT WILSON IN. It made a good picture.

Much else besides, too tedious to enumerate. Book reviewing, for instance, always buoyed up by Dr. Johnson's sage remark about the novels of Congreve, that he'd sooner praise them than read them. And memoirs, memoirs without end. Right Honourable gents who have touched life at many points; admirals, generals and air-marshals with battles to fight again, learned judges with yet one more summing-up to offer, lechers recalling old loves and teenagers looking forward to new ones. And obituaries, piled high in the morgue, one's own among them, reflecting like geological strata the ups and downs of fortune! Hard not to sing at the work as one tapped out new ones. How so-and-so, alive and kicking, had been cut off in his prime — statesmen, churchmen, dons, captains of industry, trade union bosses, one and all leaving a gap that never would be filled; some scene, House of Commons, cathedral, college high table, boardroom, Transport House, that, without them, would never be the same again.

And then, panels. Dear God, the panels! Seated round the microphone, a professor of sociology from Leeds, a resonant life peeress with a moustache, a nondescript clergyman heavy with sideburns, and myself. 'Do the Panel Think?' Oh we do, we do. Thinkers all! Participation in such panels over the years is probably responsible for a nightmare that regularly afflicts me. I'm in a BBC studio, deep underground. Above, the mushroom clouds are forming, and the last traces of civilised life are disappearing. In the studio we are engrossed in a discussion about the alarming rise in juvenile delinquency. 'What is needed,' the life peeress is resonantly contending, 'is more and *better* education.' 'If only,' she goes on, 'the age of consent could be lowered to nine, and the school age raised to nineteen; if only birth pills could be distributed to Brownies with their morning milk, and sex education begin in the play school, and *Lady Chatterly's Lover* get into the comics, all would yet be well.' It is at this point that I always wake up screaming, so that I never know how the discussion proceeds, and what is its outcome, if any.

But, of course, the essential quest has been for news. This is the Unholy Grail, the ultimate fantasy on which the whole structure of the media is founded. Shouted down a telephone, tapped out on a teleprinter, carried breathlessly to the stone to catch the edition, beamed by satellite through the stratosphere, whispered confidentially in a favoured ear, set forth in communiqués for one and all, spoken into microphones, recorded on film and video — the nothingness of news. 'Ten thousand people shouting the same thing make it false, even if it happens to be true,' Kirkegaard says. News is ten million people induced to think the same thing, which makes it a thousand times more false in the unlikely event of its happening to be true.

My first acquaintance with news-gathering and processing was in Cairo in the early twenties when I was teaching at the university there. Academic standards were low, and my duties not exacting; the students were frequently on strike, and anyway barely understood English. Added to this, they were liable to be stupefied with hashish. Incidentally, I find it strange now, looking back, to recall that in that far-off time there were no reputable English residents in Cairo, or Egyptians for that matter, who would for a moment have considered hashish as being other than an utterly deplorable addiction; whereas today, some five decades later, eminent personages come forward to insist, not merely that it is harmless, but positively beneficial.

With so much leisure on my hands, and an in-born chronic mania to use words and express opinions, I started writing articles on Egyptian politics, dominated in those days by the pashas and beys of the Mohammed Ali Club, King Fuad with his Salvador Dali-like moustache, and Lord Lloyd, the British High Commissioner, on whose shoulder, he told me when subsequently we became acquainted, the King would sometimes weep. Planning and writing these articles, I all too easily acquired facility in the use of the fraudulent language of news; reporting, for instance, that opinion among Egyptians was hardening and that, conscious of their newly-acquired nationhood, they would assuredly never be content with anything less than full national sovereignty based on universal suffrage democracy. The words seemed to pick themselves out on my typewriter keyboard of their own volition, and then to fly like homing pigeons in at the windows of the *Guardian* office in Cross Street, Manchester, whither I in due course followed them myself.

In Manchester I was initiated into another aspect of news-handling — editorialising. Seated at my typewriter, with only a brick wall for outlook, I became expert at unravelling in a few ill-chosen words what was afoot at an Indian Round-Table Conference; likewise, at denouncing a new hexagonal gasometer calculated to mar Manchester's delectable skyline, or exposing the sinister implications of a lately-formed government in Athens. Our editorial offerings, whether shorts or longs, were expected to conclude with a general expression of goodwill, which usually took the form of a hope that somehow or other moderate men of all shades of opinion would draw together to ensure that wiser counsels might yet prevail. These labours soon palled, especially as the world seemed increasingly to be full of immoderate men whose counsels grew ever crazier.

The alternative, I decided, was Moscow, where, Lincoln Steffens averred, he had seen the future and it worked. I, too, wanted to see the future and make sure that it really was working, and to this end got myself sent to Moscow as the *Guardian's* correspondent there. In Moscow, as I soon discovered, news was confined to what appeared in the newspaper

Pravda — a word which, as is well known, means 'truth', and so, in the circumstances, had ironical undertones for the local populace. Each morning my Russian secretary read through to me in a sing-song voice her English translation of news stories and articles appearing in this truly appallingly boring publication. The only comparable experience I can recall was when the late Professor Namier read aloud to me very slowly and laboriously an interminable article from the *Times Literary Supplement*. If I detected anything in my secretary's melancholy chant that might be of interest to English readers, I stopped her while I made a few notes. Later, out of these notes, I concocted a message for the *Guardian*, which had to be written in a weird telegraphese to economise on wordage: ADDRESSING ALLUNION CENTRAL EXECUTIVE COMMITTEE YESTERDAY MOLOTOV SAID SOVGOV UNFAVOURED PROJECTED AMERICAN COMMISSION PROBE RECOGNITION . . . The message had to be taken to the censors, one of whom was required to append his initials for it to be accepted at the telegraph office. In those days the censors were all Russian Jews who had lived abroad and then returned to Russia after the Revolution; jovial, wily men with thin tapering beards. One of them, named Podolsky, said to me once, after reading through a message I had submitted to him: 'You can't send this because it's true' — an interesting comment which would provide an apt refrain in a musical called *News*, if one on such a theme were ever to be produced. It was Podolsky who passed the only indubitably true sentence I ever telegraphed — perhaps that ever has been telegraphed — out of Moscow. At the time I was standing in for one of the news agency men and received a request: SEND SOONEST REACTION SOVMASSES LAVISH SCALE ENTERTAINING THEIR EMBASSIES ABROAD, to which I replied, without consulting so much as a single moujik: REACTION SOVMASSES ARDENT WISH GET NEAREST BUFFET. Podolsky, like nearly all his colleagues

in the Foreign Press Department during my time in Mosc
in due course disappeared into a labour camp, never to be s
again. I trust I did not expedite his departure.

After Moscow, Geneva, where the League of Nations
drowning in a positive maelstrom of news, to be reincarn;
as the United Nations, which may be said to be awash ir
ocean of news. Then off to India, to Simla, the mountain e
where the Viceroy and his court and government resorte(
the hot summer months. The Viceroy, a slight, frail man
grey topper and grey frock-coat, seemed infinitely rem
logistically and in every way, from his four hundred mil
subjects in the steaming plains below; but he, too, had new
dispense on behalf of his Government — of constituti(
reforms that would never be implemented, of a self-goveri
All-India Federation that would never come to pass, of
genious franchise arrangements never to emerge from t
White Paper. It was a relief to get back to Fleet Street, ther
join a team producing gossip paragraphs for an evening pa
This was yet another form of news, to be gleaned from
doings and sayings of a stage army of celebrities of one sort
another, who could be relied on to put in an appearanc
political and social occasions. It was easier, I discovered
invent what they did and said than to follow them around
eavesdrop. After all, they were phantom people, such stu;
dreams are made of, so that actually encountering them in
flesh could not but spoil the story. The ideal arrangement
to be on Christian name terms with them without ever mal
their acquaintance.

Not even war, when it came in 1939, delivered me from
servitude to the media. First I was drafted into the Ministr
Information to write articles calculated to promote our
effort at home, and to lure into our camp waverers abr
When, in distress, I joined the army as a private, I soon fo
myself engaged in Intelligence duties, Intelligence being
media in wartime disguise. It involved, I found, the same

quest for news but carried to yet further extremes of fantasy. As a news-gatherer I had often been expected to make bricks without straw, but as an Intelligence agent it was a matter of growing lemons without a tree.

With the war over, I once more returned to Fleet Street, but soon grew restless there, and managed to persuade the *Daily Telegraph* to send me to Washington D.C., as fifteen years previously I had persuaded the *Guardian* to send me to Moscow. In those post-war years Washington was the centre round which the world's magnetic field of news arranged itself. The huge newspapers were bursting at the seams with news; in my tiny office in the National Press Building two ticker-tape machines continuously spewed forth news agency copy on yellow paper which in my absence was liable to accumulate on the floor in unseemly piles — the slagheaps of my trade. In Moscow the trouble had been the total absence of news; in Washington there was a super abundance. At all hours of the day and night the stream of news flowed on; the very air was heavy with it as radio and television stations transmitted their bulletins every hour on the hour round the clock. News was endlessly analysed, synthesised, liquidised, to form a single soothing brew — *Newzak*, a melange of happenings and sayings as *Muzak* is of tunes and melodies, the two together, now the *Muzak*, now the *Newzak* (but which was which?) comforting and soothing motorists driving from nowhere to nowhere along the motorways, six lanes a side, with the tarmac stretching interminably ahead, a cigarette to pull on, a suit from the cleaners swinging gently to and fro on its hanger, pressing ever onwards through the little towns — Athens, Windsor, Venice, Babylon — each one signalised by four neon signs shining in the darkness: FOOD, GAS, BEAUTY, DRUGS, the four pillars of our twentieth-century way of life.

It was in the light of this long involvement in the fantasy of the media that I came to envisage the Devil making a fourth attempt to suborn Jesus after the failure of his three previous attempts in the wilderness. I saw it in this wise: Our Lord is going about in Galilee, teaching and healing and proclaiming his kingdom of love, in contradistinction to the Devil's kingdom of power. In media terms, he is just another crackpot, of which there were any number around at that time in that part of the world. Had I been a journalist there I should, I am sure, have spent my time hanging about King Herod's palace, following the comings and goings of Pilate, trying to find out what was afoot in the Sanhedrin; the cameras would have been set up in Caesarea, not in Galilee, still less on Golgotha. Not so the Devil; he wouldn't have been fooled, well aware that the Incarnation represented the greatest threat he had ever encountered, and that Jesus was the most formidable assailant who had ever confronted him. The Devil knows the ways of the world better than most, if only because he has had a big hand in shaping them. Likewise, he can foresee the developments and dénouements of history — a show he mounts; his own special spectacular, and when seasonable, pantomine. So, he decides to have yet another go at tempting Jesus.

The first temptation, it will be recalled, was to persuade Jesus to turn stones into bread, thereby abolishing hunger, coping with the alleged population explosion, and otherwise benefiting mankind. The second was to induce him to jump off the top of the Temple without coming to any harm, thereby achieving celebrity and so attracting the world's attention to what he had to say. The third was to accept the kingdoms of the earth at the hands of the Devil, in whose gift they were, and are, thereby acquiring the requisite power to set up a Kingdom of Heaven here on earth, wherein mankind could live happily and prosperously ever after — a super-welfare state, a co-operative commonwealth, a dictatorship of the proletariat, any brand whatsoever, according to fancy. Jesus turned down all three offers, recognising that to provide unlimited bread would induce men to believe that they could live by bread alone — a

preview of our affluent society; that seeking celebrity by exploit-
ing God's concern for him would induce men to see themselves
as gods and worship themselves accordingly, and that acceptance of the kingdoms of the earth would involve opting for
Caesar rather than God, and so render his ministry meaningless.
As Dostoevsky shows so brilliantly in the famous scene in *The
Brothers Karamazov* between the Grand Inquisitor and the
returned Christ, what was really at risk in the temptations was
the greatest gift Jesus brought us when he came into the world
— our true freedom: what St. Paul called the glorious liberty of
the children of God, the only lasting liberty there is.

Has any generation of men had it demonstrated to them more
forcibly than ours that Dostoevsky's analysis of the temptations
is correct? Have we not been shown in the most dramatic manner
how economic miracles end in servitude to economics? How the
glorification of Man leads infallibly to the servitude of men, and
his liberation through power to one variety or another of Gulag
Archipelago? This notwithstanding, after the passage of twenty
centuries, what Jesus turned down so resolutely in the wilderness tends to find many takers today on his behalf among his
ostensible followers, who are ready enough to cheer him to the
skies as a superstar, elect him with a huge majority to be the
Honourable Member for Galilee South, sign him up with the
urban guerrillas, and adapt his Sermon on the Mount to be a
Sermon on the Barricades.

Let us, then, try and imagine how the fourth temptation
might have come about. Some Roman tycoon, enormously rich,
an impresario of the games, Lucius Gradus the Elder, let us
call him, happens to be passing through Galilee and hears
Jesus speaking and teaching there. An obscure and insignificant
event in itself — just a nondescript crowd gathered round a
teacher, himself of little account according to Gradus's reckoning. Somehow, however, the scene impresses him, as do the
speaker's words. Their very extravagance holds his attention:
how God's love falls with crazy abundance on the just and the

unjust alike, how we must love our enemies and do good to
them that harm us, how if an eye offends it must be plucked out
and if a limb it must be amputated. If, Gradus reasons, such
verbal prodigality holds his attention, why shouldn't it have
an equally strong impact on the general public? Properly presented, he feels, this Jesus's line of talk might have a big appeal,
and the man himself prove to be possessed of potential star, if
not superstar, quality.

As a start, Gradus decides to instruct his representatives in
Jerusalem to 'puff Jesus'. Then, when he gets back to Rome,
he puts it to his associates that they should bring Jesus to
Rome. Maybe, too, it would be a good idea to bring over one
or two of his followers to participate in the act. One of them
was a man he'd heard of called the Baptist, a very picturesque
guy with a great tangled beard and dressed in a camel's-hair
shirt with a leather girdle round him. He'd be great on the set in
his desert get-up. Just now he was said to be doing a stretch
in prison, but Gradus felt sure that the Procurator — Pontius
something-or-other — or 'King' Herod could easily be induced
to let him out for the show. It should be put on, of course, in
prime time, and not, it went without saying, in the religious slot.
That would kill it stone dead from the word go. For the set
they'd have fountains playing, a lush atmosphere, with organ
music, a good chorus-line, if possible from Delphi, and some
big names from the games — gladiators in full rig; also, if
possible, priests and priestesses from the Aphrodite Temple, and
maybe from some of the Eastern cults becoming so popular
with the young. Jesus himself would need something special
in the way of a robe, and a hair-do and beard trim. He'd be the
central figure, naturally, but for safety's sake his words would
have to be put on autocue. Here a doubt seized Gradus. Could
Jesus read? On reflection he decides that it doesn't really
matter. The show would have to be mimed anyway, and because of the language difficulty they'd have to use lip-sinc. To
avoid any impression of bigotry, there would be readings from

different scriptures, including Hebrew, of course, and a discussion running to eight to ten minutes for which they'd get over some teachers and students from the Philosophy School in Athens — always good value.

Would Jesus agree? Gradus laughs at the mere notion of a refusal. How could he possibly refuse what would enable him to reach a huge public, right across the Roman Empire, instead of the rag, tag and bobtail lot following him around in Galilee? In propositioning Jesus, Gradus goes on, it should be stressed that there would be no intrusion of unsuitable commercials; just a very reputable sponsor — say, the highly-respected public relations consultancy, Lucifer Inc. No more than: 'This programme comes to you by the courtesy of Lucifer Inc.,' at the beginning and after the credits at the end. 'Why,' Gradus says banging on the table, 'it'll put him on the map, launch him off on a tremendous career as a worldwide evangelist, spread his teaching throughout the civilised world, and beyond. He'd be crazy to turn it down.'

Jesus, who, in Gradus's terms, *was* crazy, did turn it down all the same, as he had the other three temptations. He was concerned with truth and reality, Gradus with fantasy and images. In any case, Jesus, as he well knew, was involved in another scenario than Gradus's altogether; no less than the great drama of the Incarnation, the Passion and the Resurrection. It may seem extraordinary to us now that this drama, and all it has meant for mankind in enhancing our mortal existence, should have been carried, without benefit of media, first from Judea to Asia Minor, and thence to Europe to spread through the whole Roman Empire. How, when the Roman Empire finally disintegrated, it provided the basis for a new great civilisation — Christendom, whose legatees we are. How all the greatest artists, poets and musicians dedicated their genius to celebrating it, and how majestic cathedrals were built to enshrine it, and religious orders founded to serve it. How mystics spent their lives exploring it, and how for centuries it was the driving force

of all the greatest human endeavour, the source of the brightest
and most far-reaching hopes ever to be entertained by the
human mind, and the most sublime purposes ever to be undertaken by the human will. How the sheer creativity released by
this drama, fabulous in its range, extended to every field of
exploration, from the illimitable expanses of space to the tiniest
particle of matter. What a feat of communication is there to
contemplate!

We, on the other hand, have developed our fantastic technology of communication whereby words are transmitted round
the world faster than sound, with satellites to pick them up and
send them on their way; likewise pictures, even of planets
billions of miles away, brought to our television screens. Every
imaginable and unimaginable facility exists for making ourselves heard and seen. But have we anything to say? Anything
to show? I love the irony that God in his infinite mercy injects
into all our feats, to keep us humble lest we should harbour the
fatal illusion of being gods ourselves, and to keep us laughing
lest we should take ourselves seriously. Besides the steeples
climbing into the sky he plants the gargoyles grinning down at
the earth — a celestial contribution to the theatre of the absurd.
It may break the heart of an editor of *Punch* vainly trying to be
funny about a world that proves to be incorrigibly funnier than
anything he can invent, but it is also sublime, demonstrating,
as it does, that our amazing technology has a built-in *reductio
ad absurdum*, whereas the Word that became flesh, and dwelt
among us, full of grace and truth, in the most literal sense,
speaks for itself.

For the author's replies to questions posed by those attending this lecture,
please turn to page 81.

THE DEAD SEA VIDEO
TAPES

IN MY FIRST lecture I considered the fantasy world the media project and in which they enmesh us, in contradistinction to the reality of Christ's Kingdom proclaimed during his ministry on earth, and open still, as it has been throughout the Christian centuries, to all who truly seek it. As it seems to me, perhaps because I have so often had occasion, professionally, to cross from one to the other, and know from long experience how wide, and widening, is the gap between them, these two worlds are drawing ever more implacably apart. Or is it just that being old and near the end of my days, the contrast between the reality I see ahead and the fantasy I shall soon be leaving behind for ever seems to be the more marked — like looking down on a smog-infested city set in a sunlit plain. In any case, I have a longing past conveying to stay, during such time as remains to me in this world, with the reality of Christ, and to use whatever gifts of persuasion I may have to induce others to see that they must at all costs hold on to that reality; lash themselves to it, as in the old days of sail, sailors would lash themselves to the mast when storms blew up and the seas were rough. For, indeed, without a doubt, storms and rough seas lie ahead.

Let me add this, speaking as someone who has lived for some years in what I call the NTBR belt, that is to say, belonging to the category of people of sixty-five years and over who in our humane society are liable to have marked on their medical cards, if they get ill and go to hospital, NTBR, which means 'Not To Be Resuscitated'. Being, then, well past my allotted span of three score years and ten, as the old do, I often wake up in the night and feel myself, in some curious way, half in and half out of my body, so that I seem to be hovering between the battered old carcass that I can see between the sheets, and seeing in the darkness and in the distance a glow in the sky, the lights of Augustine's City of God. In that condition, when it seems just a toss-up whether I return into my body to live out another day, or make off, there are two particular conclusions, two extraordinarily sharp impressions, that come to me. The first is of the incredible beauty of our earth — its colours and its shapes, its smells and its creatures; of the enchantment of human love and companionship, and of the blessed fulfilment provided by human work and human procreation. And the second, a certainty surpassing all words and thoughts, that as an infinitesimal particle of God's creation I am a participant in his purposes, which are loving and not malign, creative and not destructive, orderly and not chaotic, universal and not particular. And in that certainty, a great peace and a great joy.

I open my remarks this evening in this strain because I am conscious of having perhaps dwelt too intensively in my first lecture on the sinister aspects of the media, and on the hopelessness of expecting any good in Christian terms to come of them. So, let me add that Christianity is, and has always been, and always will be, not just essentially a religion of hope, but in itself, the most stupendous hope the world has ever known. Only Incarnate God would have dared to hold out to us all, mere men and women of every sort and condition, sweet mongols and pundits and professors and beauty queens, the sick and the well, the stupid and the clever, those who stumble equally with those who lend an arm, whoever and whatever we may be, a hope of being involved in a destiny set in eternity and encompassing the universe. Imagine telling caterpillars that they are destined to become butterflies. No A-levels needed, not even literacy tests, the only qualification being faith in becoming a butterfly, and lo, the poor crawler is flying, the worm has sprouted wings! More exquisitely shaped and decorated, more efficient in their fragility than any mortal craftsman could possibly manage. Carrying the image further, I imagine a TV panel of caterpillars discussing the implications of the prophecy that they were destined to become butterflies, with one of them, the genus *Popilio Soperino*, insisting that what the prophecy really signifies is that all caterpillars should join the Labour Party.

The fact is, of course, that the media themselves, with all their power of persuasion and corruption, are really rather a trivial, and at best second-rate set-up. They can no more keep Christ out than the Emperor Nero could keep the words of the Apostle Paul from spreading themselves throughout an already ramshackle Roman empire. Nor, by the same token, can the media keep him in — in their *Jesus Christ Superstar*, or their *Stars on Sunday*, or any other variety of stardom they can devise. It is as ridiculous to talk about the beneficent influence of the media in widening peoples' horizons, opening windows on to the world, and all that sort of humbug, as it is to blame the media for all our present ills — an error, I admit, I am prone to fall into myself. The media in themselves have no power, any more than nuclear weapons have; both have power only to the extent that they can influence and exploit the weaknesses and the wretchedness of men — their carnality which makes them vulnerable to the pornographer, their greed and vanity which delivers them into the hands of the advertiser, their credulity which makes them so susceptible to the fradulent prospectuses of ideologues and politicians; above all, their arrogance, which induces them to fall so readily for any agitator or agitation, revolutionary or counter-revolutionary, which brings to their nostrils the acrid scent of power.

Here let me quote some words by Simone Weil, in my opinion one of the most luminous intelligences of our time, words which I have often meditated upon, and which are very relevant to my subject:

Nothing is so beautiful, nothing is so continually fresh and surprising, so full of sweet and perpetual ecstasy, as the good; no desert is so dreary, monotonous and boring as evil. But with fantasy it's the other way round. Fictional good is boring and flat, while fictional evil is varied, intriguing, attractive and full of charm.

These words were written a decade or so before television had been developed to attract its huge audiences all over the world, becoming the greatest fabricator and conveyor of fantasy that has ever existed. Its offerings, as it seems to me, bear out the point Simone Weil makes to a quite remarkable degree. For in them, it is almost invariably *eros* rather than *agape* that provides all the excitement; celebrity and success rather than a broken and a contrite heart that are held up as being pre-eminently desirable; Jesus Christ in lights on Broadway rather than Jesus Christ on the cross who gets a folk hero's billing.

Good and evil, after all, provide the basic theme of the drama of our mortal existence, and in this sense may be compared with the positive and negative points which generate an electric current; transpose the points, and the current fails, the lights go out, darkness falls, and all is confusion. So it is with us. The transposition of good and evil in the world of fantasy created by the media leaves us with no sense of any moral order in the universe, and without this, no order whatsoever, social, political, economic or any other, is ultimately attainable. There is only chaos. To break out of the fantasy, to rediscover the reality of good and evil, and therefore the order which informs all creation — this is the freedom that the Incarnation made available, that the Saints have celebrated and that the Holy Spirit has sanctified.

No doubt my strong feelings about the media and heightened sense of the ill consequences of the eight years of a working life that a majority of our citizens dedicate to the TV screen, are products of my own telelife. Indeed, I had the idea originally of calling these lectures: 'The Confessions of a Justified Communicator'. There is something very terrible in becoming an image, which is what, of course, being filmed or video taped involves. You see yourself on a screen, walking, talking, moving about, posturing, and it is not you. Or is it you, and the you looking at you, someone else? All very confusing and disturbing, making one understand the *doppelgänger* horror stories, and think with new insight of the Second Commandment: 'Thou shalt not make unto thee any graven image, or any likeness of anything that is in heaven above or that is in the earth beneath, or that is in the water under the earth.' It is the one of the Ten Commandments I have always thought of as being rather easily evaded, and therefore as the least exacting. Now I am inclined to feel differently. An image on a screen may not be graven, but it is indubitably an image, and carries with it sinister undertones of narcissism. To infringe the Second Commandment by making oneself into a graven image would seem to be to double the offence, and helps to explain why those involved in this existence in duplicate often bear upon them marks of strain and woe. I well remember the tragic state of mind of Gilbert Harding shortly before his death. And there have been others, even some suicides. In the days when I used to look at television in the evening, it quite often happened that I fell asleep. This, as I have observed, is liable to happen to whole families: the set is in full activity, and all the viewers sleeping — surely a parable picture for our time. Once, sleeping before a television screen, I woke up to find myself on it. The experience was quite terrifying — like some awful nightmare to which only someone like Edgar Allan Poe or Dostoevsky could do justice.

In the light of all this, I ask myself whether orthodox Jews, and adherents of sects like the Mennonities, are so wide of the mark in resolutely eschewing being photographed altogether. I remember once going with cameras into a district of New York largely inhabited by ultra-orthodox Jews, and how, on our appearance, everyone ran for cover. The opposite, I need scarcely say, is the usual response; the cameras draw people to them like bees round a honey pot. It seems very strange now, but I well recall how, in the early days of television, we used to have to persuade and coax people into the studios; even politicians would be quite hesitant in agreeing to come in front of the cameras. How different things are today! I feel quite sure that if an advertisement were to be put in *The Times* to the effect that Members of either House of Parliament who walked barefoot with a rope round their necks from John o'Groats to Shepherd's Bush would be accorded ten minutes of prime time on television, the roads would be thronging with Noble Lords and Honourable Members, attired and accoutred as required.

It is significant, I think, that Jesus, in dealing with the mentally afflicted, for whom he always showed a particular concern, restored them to sanity by getting rid of their demonic alter ego, thereby making them one person again and delivering them from images. He, the supreme antidote to fantasy and master of reality, as it were, extricated them from the television screen and brought them back into life. I thought of this when I had occasion once to take Mother Theresa into a New York television studio for her to appear in the *Morning Show*, a programme which helps Americans from coast to coast to munch their breakfast cereal and gulp down their breakfast coffee. She was to be interviewed by a man we could see on a studio monitor in living colour, with a drooping green moustache, a purple nose and scarlet hair. It was the first time Mother Teresa had been in an American television studio, and so she was quite unprepared for the constant interruptions for commercials. As it happened, surely as a result of divine intervention, all the commercials that particular morning were to do with different varieties of packaged food, recommended as being non-fattening and non-nourishing. Mother Teresa looked at them with a kind of wonder, her own constant preoccupation being, of course, to find the wherewithal to nourish the starving and put some flesh on human skeletons. It took some little time for the irony of the situation to strike her. When it did, she remarked, in a perfectly audible voice: 'I see that Christ is needed in television studios.' A total silence descended on all present, and I fully expected the lights to go out and the floor manager to drop dead. Reality had momentarily intruded into one of the media's mills of fantasy — an unprecedented occurrence. Somehow it gave me an extraordinarily vivid sense of what it must have been like all those years ago in the Temple at Jerusalem, when the money-changers were chased out, and their tables overturned. In the studio normal proceedings for the *Morning Show* were soon resumed, just as I am sure the money-changers were back in their places the following day. Indeed, they are there still. Both incidents, however, bear out the saying with which Solzhenitsyn concludes his Nobel lecture: 'One word of truth outweighs the world.'

This business of being an image was brought home to me in more frivolous terms quite recently when I had been abroad for some time, and therefore had not been seen at all on television. To my amazement, the people in my village greeted me with the old familiar cry, ejaculated in an admonitory tone of voice: 'We saw you on the telly!' I explained that this was impossible, and then it turned out that there is a man called Mike Yarwood who does an impersonation of me. Clearly, he makes more of an impression on the screen than I can hope to achieve myself — a humbling thought! Then there was a newspaper competition; one of those very easy ones, like the recently-introduced no-fail examinations. Readers were simply given a list of names, and asked to specify which of them were of real people and which were fictitious. Well, I was one of the names, and I am happy to be able to report that sixty-one per cent of the paper's readers thought I was a real person — quite a satisfactory result, which put me two points ahead of the Reverend Ian Paisley.

Another experience of being an image was becoming a wax-work in Madame Tussaud's Exhibition. This was a distinction which came my way some years ago, and led to my being put in a room beside no less a person than Twiggy, in the process of having a bath as a matter of fact. In the same room, presumably to ensure that everything was as it should be, there loomed up the massive figure of General de Gaulle. I used to toy with the notion that perhaps it might be possible to change places with my waxwork and spend a few days quietly in Baker Street with Twiggy and the General, leaving my waxwork to function on my behalf. However, the project proved impracticable, and now I learn from my grandchildren, who are my great informants on this subject, that I have been moved from Twiggy's side to stand by the entrance to the Exhibition, which seems to me to be a sure sign that I shall shortly be taken away and melted down. For a connoisseur of images like myself, the most interesting part of the whole experience was being taken on a tour of the Exhibition's nether regions, where there is a remarkabe collection of bits and pieces of waxworks; items such as Gandhi's leg, Sophia Loren's bust, a famous Archbishop of Canterbury's rump — oddments like that casually lying about. What fascinated me most, however, was a collection of no less than six heads of Harold Wilson, who was Prime Minister at the time. I asked why six heads, and was told, believe it or not, that it was because during his period of office his head had been growing steadily bigger, so that it was necessary to re-do it from time to time. Why, you may ask, keep all the six used heads? Because, it was calculated, out of office his head might begin shrinking again, and the old heads come in handy.

This evening's chairman, Sir Brian Young, spoke about my having had my aerials removed; and that is true. I've had them removed, and I feel much better for it. Their removal, as far as I'm concerned, amounts to a kind of moral equivalent of a prostate operation. What finally decided me to give up looking at television was a series of programmes called *Family*, billed in the *Radio Times* — that compendium of ineptitude — as a 'real life documentary'. To suppose that life could really be lived followed about everywhere by a camera, I decided, really did represent the ultimate fantasy, not just of television, but of life itself. Furthermore, it goes without saying that the allegedly real life of the family in question, as presented on the screen, was calculated to devalue the whole concept of family life in Christian terms.

Was this the conscious purpose of those concerned in the production and editing of the programme? Not so, I should say. From the lowest dregs of the media, like *Penthouse* or *Forum*, to the dizzy heights of Radio 3 lectures on Milton's politics or Dante's imagery, from *Steptoe and Son* and *Upstairs Downstairs* to Clark's *Civilisation* and Bronowski's *Ascent of Man*, through the whole media gamut, there runs a consensus or orthodoxy which is, within broad limits, followed, and in some degree, imposed. Certainly, any marked deviation other than in terms of eccentricity — the 'Alf Garnett' syndrome, for instance — is at some point, or by some means, disallowed. At the same time, there is every reason to believe that this happens of itself. People are not hand-picked for this or that job because they fall in with the consensus. Nor are they, in any way that I know of, pressurised to fall in with it in the course of their work. All the same, they are consensus-orientated, if not -fixated. One way and another, I know a lot of people working in the media; on newspapers, magazines, in news agencies, in radio and television, and believe me, I should have the utmost difficulty in naming more than a handful whose views are not absolutely predictable on matters like abortion, the population explosion, family planning, anything whatever to do with contemporary *mores*, as well as aesthetics, politics and economics, who will not say more or less the same thing in the same words about, say, Nixon, or Solzhenitsyn, or apartheid, or Rhodesia. If, as sometimes happens, someone from the media whom I don't happen to know comes down to interview me, or consult with me, I make certain assumptions about his or her views, as falling in with the consensus, and am seldom proved mistaken.

This, in my experience, applies as much to the religious broadcasting department as any other; if not more so. Wide variations here are most unusual; Roman Catholic priests who wholeheartedly support *Humanae Vitae*, or evangelicals who believe unequivocally in the Ten Commandments, are little in evidence. Consensus-making and -promoting, I should say, is to be seen historically as an instinctive preparation for some sort of conformist-collectivist society which lies ahead whatever may happen, all that is in doubt being the precise ideology which will characterise it. What is beyond question is that consensus power has sufficed, for instance, in the United States to bring about an American defeat in the Vietnam War, to unseat a President and damage, perhaps fatally, the institution of the Presidency, besides dismantling the CIA, America's Intelligence arm, such as it is. In this country, the same force has discredited and rendered nugatory the whole structure of Christian ethics, and succeeded in holding up to ridicule and contempt all who continue to assert that chastity is a beautiful and necessary virtue, that eroticism only has validity in the context of lasting love, which is its condition, and procreation, which is its purpose, and that making films like *Rosemary's Baby* accessible to the young and immature by showing them on television, is an outrage. In surveying the future of the media, it should be realised that the ever-expanding television schedules cannot be filled except with the help of old movies, which means that the more successful films now being shown in the cinemas will find their way almost automatically on to the television screen. As many of these belong to a category that up till quite recently would have found an outlet only in squalid Soho or Montmartre dives, it may be assumed that before very long children will be watching what has hitherto been reserved for the sick, the perverse and the depraved. Only the most naïve or the most hypocritical among media bosses will be able to persuade themselves that, in the normal conditions of family viewing, children can be prevented from seeing such films by showing them late in the evening.

Thinking of this seemingly deliberate corruption of the young and innocent for money, or, in the case of the BBC, even more contemptibly, for ratings, it occurred to me that the following would be a useful exercise, though it requires a Jonathan Swift to explore its possibilities fully and with appropriate irony. Let us imagine that, somehow or other, a whole lot of contemporary pabulum — video tape and film of television programmes with accompanying news footage and advertisements, copies of newspapers and magazines, tapes of pop groups and other cacophonies, best-selling novels, a selection of successful films, recordings of political speeches, exhortations, comedies and talk shows, and other recordings of the diversions, interests and entertainments of our time — gets preserved, like the Dead Sea Scrolls, in some remote salt cave. Then, centuries, or maybe millennia, later, when our civilisation will long since have joined the others that once were, and now can only be patiently reconstructed out of dusty ruins, incomprehensible hieroglyphics and other residuary relics, archaeologists discover the cave and set about sorting out its contents, trying to deduce from them the sort of people we were and how we lived.

What, we may wonder, would the archaeologists make of us? Materially so rich and so powerful, spiritually so impoverished and so fear-ridden, having made such remarkable inroads into discovering the secrets of nature and into unravelling the mechanisms of our material environment, beginning to explore, and perhaps to colonise, the universe itself, developing the means to produce in more or less unlimited quantities everything we could possibly need or desire, to transmit swifter than light every thought, smile or word that could possibly entertain, instruct or delight us, disposing of treasure beyond calculation, opening up possibilities beyond envisaging, yet seemingly haunted by a panic fear of becoming too numerous, to the point that there would be no room on the earth for its inhabitants and an insufficiency of food to sustain them. On the one hand, a neurotic passion to increase consumption, promoted by every sort of fatuous persuasion among the technologically advanced people of the Western world; on the other, ever-increasing hunger and want among the rest of mankind. Never, the archaeologists will surely conclude, was any generation of men, ostensibly intent upon the pursuit of happiness and plenty, more advantageously placed to attain it, who yet, with apparent deliberation, took the opposite course, towards chaos, not order, towards breakdown, not stability, towards death, destruction and darkness, not life, creativity and light. An ascent that ran downhill, plenty that turned into a wasteland, a cornucopia whose abundance made hungry, a death-wish inexorably unfolded. This, as it seems to me, cannot but be the archaeologists' general conclusion from the material available to them.

All those preposterous advertisements, technically speaking the best camera work of all, beautifully produced, in the magazines, on the glossiest of glossy paper, on film or video tape, flawless, commending this or that cigarette as conducive to romantic encounters by a waterfall, some potion or cosmetic sure to endow any face, hands or limbs with irresistible loveliness, or medicament which will give sleep, cure depression, remove headaches, acidity, body odour and other ills — can it have been, the archaeologists will ask themselves, in the light of the almost inconceivable credulity required, and apparently forthcoming, some long since forgotten religious cult? A cult of consumption; the supermarkets with soft music playing, its temples; the so-persuasive voices, 'Buy this! Eat this! Wear this! Drink this!' of priests and priestesses; the transformation wrought by adopting such a diet, using such gadgets, stretching out on such a bed, the miracles; with *Muzak* for plainsong, computers for oracles, cash-registers ringing in the offertory — so, they will conclude, the worship of the great god Consumption was conducted, with seemly reverence and dedication. There were even religious orders, with prodigies in the way of asceticism being performed in the interest of slimming and otherwise beautifying the male and female person.

Contrasting with this apparently flourishing cult, the archaeologists would detect vestigial traces of an earlier faith called Christianity, which had become, it seemed, largely associated with social and political causes. Thus, the prevailing Christian ethic, in so far as one could be detected at all, was based on the concept that human beings were victims of their circumstances; in the nomenclature used by some moralists, 'situational'. In the folk stories, plentifully represented in the film and video footage, misbehaviour was almost invariably shown as being due to adverse living conditions, or to mental and moral states beyond the control of the individuals concerned; never to deliberate wrongdoing, so that the notion of sin seemed to have largely disappeared, and virtue, in so far as the concept still existed, to have found expression exclusively in social acts and attitudes. If any of the archaeologists were interested enough, they could trace the adjustments and distortions of the original Christian texts — always, it goes without saying, ostensibly in the interests of clarification — to conform with the concept of Jesus as a revolutionary leader and reformer, a superior Barabbas or Che Guevara, whose kingdom indubitably was of this world, finding in this textual and doctrinal adjustment an example of the infinite ingenuity of the human mind in shaping everlasting truths to conform with temporal exigencies. It might amuse one or other of the archaeologists with a Gibbonian turn of mind to note how easily hallowed sayings were turned round to signify their opposites: as, that it is absolutely essential to lay up treasure on earth, in the shape of an ever-increasing Gross National Product; that the flesh lusts with the spirit, and the spirit with the flesh, so that we can do whatever we have a mind to, and that he that loveth his life in this world will keep it unto life eternal, and so on.

There being nothing in the material at their disposal to suggest to the archaeologists that Christianity had any survival possibilities, especially after coming across the announcement, as they inevitably would, that God had died, their assumption that a consumption cult had replaced it as a popular faith would be reinforced. Clearly, however, they would calculate, the cult needed some doctrine to sustain it, some mystical basis to enliven it, and some redemptive process to substitute for the traditional Christian procedure of being converted or reborn.

As far as the first of these three necessities is concerned, the archaeologists would have no difficulty in identifying the appropriate doctrine — belief in progress, clearly a basic doctrine in the society under examination. The notion that human beings as individuals must necessarily get better and better is even now considered by most people to be untenable, and will doubtless still have seemed so to our archaeologists, however many centuries hence they may be examining the output of our media; but, they will note, the equivalent collective concept that social circumstances, values and behaviour had an intrinsic tendency to go on getting better and better, came to be regarded as axiomatic. On this basis, all change represents progress, and is therefore good; to change anything is *per se* to improve and reform it. Our archaeologists will have no difficulty in discovering innumerable instances of the deplorable consequences of the application of this fallacious proposition. For instance, wars, each more ferocious than the last, were confidently expected to establish once and for all the everlasting reign of peace in the world. Liberations that enslaved, revolutions that created worse tyrannies than those they replaced, divorce reform that undermined the institution of marriage, and abortion reform that resulted in ever more abortions being performed — surveying this picture of a society evidently destroying itself in the fond expectation that it was reforming itself, going inexorably backwards when it supposed itself to be advancing, how could the archaeologists conclude otherwise than that the doctrine of progress applied to man's social existence proved to be one of the most deleterious, not to say ludicrous, ever to have been envisaged?

As for some mystical content in the cult of consumption, there would be no difficulty in finding that. Sex is the mysticism of materialism, a proposition that would have been borne in upon the archaeologists when they found themselves confronted with a superabundance of erotica of every sort and description, in periodicals and books and newspapers, as in films, television programmes, plays and entertainments; a vast, obsessive catering for all tastes and ages, the lame, the halt and the infirm equally called upon to squeeze out of their frail flesh the requisite response; all impediments and restraints swept aside, no moral restrictions, no legal ones either. And then, with the coming of the birth pill, the crowning glory, the achievement of unprocreative procreation, of *coitus noninterruptus* that is also *nonfecundus*, sex at last sanctified with sterility.

As for conversion, the instrument here was clearly education in all its aspects, from tiny tots' play school to post-graduate studies, whereby the old Adam of ignorance and superstition, the blind acceptance of traditional values and ways, was to be cast off and the new twentieth-century man, erudite, enlightened, cultivated, to be born. The archaeologists will surely marvel at the high hopes placed in this educative process, seemingly regarded in the society under examination as a panacea for all ills, material, mental and spiritual; at the proliferating campuses, the ever-multiplying professors and teachers instructing more and more students in more and more subjects; at the vast sums of public money expended, and at how the pundits of the classrooms and lecture theatres were held in the highest esteem, to the point of being invited to hold forth in the television and radio studios, and even to participate in government at the highest levels. More books published, plays produced, buildings erected in a matter of decades than heretofore in the whole of recorded time; the scene set for the greatest cultural explosion of history, a Venice or a Florence on a continental scale. And the result? Instead of sages, philosopher-kings and saints, pop stars, psychiatrists and gurus. Looking for a Leonardo da Vinci or a Shakespeare, the archaeologists find only a Rolling Stone.

Surveying and weighing up the whole scene, then, will not their final conclusion be that Western man decided to abolish himself, creating his own boredom out of his own affluence, his own vulnerability out of his own strength, his own impotence out of his own erotomania, himself blowing the trumpet that brought the walls of his own city tumbling down, and, having convinced himself that he was too numerous, labouring with pill and scalpel and syringe to make himself fewer, until at last, having educated himself into imbecility, and polluted and drugged himself into stupefaction, he keeled over, a weary battered old Brontosaurus, and became extinct?

This might seem a somewhat gloomy conclusion. On the other hand, it should be remembered that archaeologists are almost invariably wrong, and it is open to anyone to draw a different conclusion from the available data in the shape of the Dead Sea Video Tapes. In any case, happily, the tapes are unlikely to survive, images being less durable than words, which have displayed a remarkable survival capacity. It was no idle boast when Jesus said, 'Heaven and earth shall pass away, but my *words* shall not pass away.' Witness the man in the labour camp described by Solzhenitsyn, who had the bunk above his, and used to climb up into it in the evening, and take old, much-folded pieces of paper out of his pocket, and read them with evident satisfaction. It turned out that they had passages from the Gospels scribbled on them, which were his solace and joy in that terrible place. He would not, I feel sure, have been similarly comforted and edified by re-runs of old footage of religious TV programmes.

So the debris and bric-à-brac of the past tell us little except that the past is over. Likewise, properly speaking, there is no such thing as history; only what Blake called 'fearful symmetry', the working out of the true nature of things. What passes for history is merely the propaganda of the victor transcribed by different hands and described from different angles. The reason the Bible can never become irrelevant or outmoded is that, unlike all other histories, in its case the victor is God. Thus, in the most literal sense, the Bible is the Word of God. If, however, it were recorded in images instead of words, it would be not the Word, but the image of God. In this sense, when the Children of Israel turned aside from God and made a golden calf, they may be said to have televised him. Similarly, in all the fantasies of our time, those who have eyes to see may read the anti-fantasy. What, for instance, more perfectly explodes the fantasy of money than inflation; of sex, than pornography; of knowledge, than education; of news, than *Newzak*; of power, than nuclear weaponry; of happiness, than its pursuit. I could go on and on. So, we have to thank God even for the media, which so convincingly and insistently demonstrate their own fantasy — to thank him indeed for everything, since everything that ever has been, is, or ever will be manifests his existence and is part of the totality of his love. Above all, we have to thank him for the Incarnation, when, *while all things were in quiet silence and that night was in the midst of her swift course, thine almighty Word leaped down from heaven out of thy royal throne.* That almighty Word was the medium, and the message was Christ.

For the author's replies to questions posed by those attending this lecture, please turn to page 89.

SEEING THROUGH THE EYE

I HAVE TRIED to show that, as I see it, the media have created, and belong to, a world of fantasy, the more dangerous because it purports to be, and is largely taken as being, the real world. Christ, on the other hand, proclaimed a new dimension of reality, so that Christendom, based on this reality, could emerge from the fantasy of a decomposing Roman civilisation.

Now we, the legatees of Christendom, are in our turn succumbing to fantasy, of which the media are an outward and visible manifestation. Thus the effect of the media at all levels is to draw people away from reality, which means away from Christ, and into fantasy, whether it be at the lowest possible level, in appeals to our cupidity, our vanity, our carnality in overtly pornographic publications and spectacles, or, in more sophisticated terms, by displaying in words or in pictures, in one context or another, the degeneracy and depravity, the divorcement from any concept of good and evil, the leaning towards perversion and violence and the sheer chaos of a society that has lost its bearings, and so is materially, morally and spiritually, adrift.

There is a passage in Pascal's *Pensées*, a book I greatly admire, that I often quote, and that seems to me highly relevant:

It is in vain, O men, that you seek within yourselves the cure for your miseries. All your insight only leads you to the knowledge that it is *not* in yourselves that you will discover the true and the good. The philosophers promised them to you, and have not been able to keep their promise. They do not know what your true good is, or what your true state is. How should they have provided you with a cure for ills which they have not even understood? Your principal maladies are pride, which cuts you off from God, and sensuality, which binds you to the earth, and they have done nothing but foster at least one of these maladies. If they have given you God for your object, it has been to pander to your pride — they have made you think you were like him, and resembled him by your nature; and those who have grasped the vanity of such a pretention have cast you down into the other abyss by making you believe that your nature is like that of the beasts of the field, and have led you to seek your good in lust, which is the lot of animals.

Substitute for 'philosophers', 'the media', and the passage is perfectly applicable today. What it says is that without God we are left with a choice of succumbing to megalomania or erotomania, and heaven knows, there is plenty going on in the world, and in the hearts and minds of contemporary men, to justify that proposition. In this retreat from reality fostered by the media, their purportedly serious offerings, especially in the field of television, are often more morally misleading and harmful than mere disgusting pornography of the kind which traffickers in this particular squalid commodity market and sell, whether in books, periodicals, films or ostensible entertainment. Such material is at least easily recognisable for what it is, except perhaps in the eyes of some deluded intellectuals, and the aspiring ones who trail along in their wake, including, alas, trendy clergymen and even bishops.

The ostensibly serious offerings of the media, on the other hand, represent a different menace precisely because they are liable to pass for being objective and authentic, whereas actually they, too, belong to the realm of fantasy. Here, the advent and exploration of visual material with the coming of the camera, has played a crucial rôle. This applies especially to news and so-called documentaries, both of which are regarded as factual, but which, in practice, are processed along with everything else in the media's fantasy-machine. Thus news becomes, not so much what has happened, as what can be seen as happening, or seems to have happened. As for documentaries, anyone who has worked on them, as I have extensively, knows that the element of simulation in them has always been considerable, and has only increased as making and directing them has become more sophisticated and technically developed. Christopher Ralling, a gifted BBC producer, in an article in the *Listener*, has expressed his concern about how documentary-makers tend more and more to venture into a no-man's-land between drama and documentary.

Four lines by Blake, like so much of what he wrote, now seem prophetic, almost as though he foresaw the coming of the camera (surely not by chance originally called 'camera obscura'!), and all it would do to us in the way of inducing us to accept fantasy as reality:

> This Life's dim windows of the soul
> Distorts the Heavens from Pole to Pole,
> And leads you to believe a lie
> When you see with, not through, the eye.

Has there ever been a more perfect instrument for seeing with rather than through the eye, than the camera? And as it has developed from bleary daguerreotypes to the latest video product, what a multitude of lies it has induced belief in, ranging between the crazy claims of advertising and the sophisticated practice of Orwell's Newspeak and Doublethink, not to mention mounting Big Brother's — or Sister's — appearances! To see through the eye is to grasp the significance of what is seen, to see it in relation to the totality of God's creation — 'All the world in a grain of sand', again to quote Blake. Just looked at, seen with the eye, which is all the camera can do, a grain of sand is but one among innumerable other identical grains, making up a sea shore or a desert. So the camera is mindless, an instrument for merely looking. As such, it is more and more taking over the media. In newspapers, magazines and colour supplements, on location, in the studio and the cutting room, increasingly the camera tends to have the last word, and, in all seriousness, it may not be very long before television production, like so much else, is almost wholly automated, with no need for any human participation, other than to maintain the machines and programme the computers.

On the prowl for news, what the camera wants is an exciting or dramatic scene which will hold viewers, thus bringing into play its own particular expertise. Pictures are all. If there is footage available of, say, an air disaster, that takes precedence as news over some other disaster — say, an earthquake — of which there is no available footage. A murder in Belfast is less newsworthy than one in Fulham because of its familiarity; famines only occur when they have been filmed, the others — and there are many, alas — are likely to continue unnoticed. News cameramen want to lead the TV news bulletins as reporters want to lead the front page of the newspapers they serve, and are always on the look-out for some scene which will photograph strikingly. The temptation to set one up is correspondingly very great. When the Berlin Wall was completed, two *vopos* — East German policemen — decided to jump off it into West Berlin. I was told by a cameraman present on the occasion that they had to jump three times before their performance was considered to be visually satisfactory.

Then there are those pictures from the Vietnam War of GI's setting fire to huts or shooting a Vietcong prisoner out of hand. The chances of such a scene presenting itself just when a camera is ready to roll, with the correct positioning, lighting and so on, is about a billion to one against. None the less, they were the camera's truth, and so valid, and incidentally in the end decisive in bringing about an ignominious American defeat. One of the most famous shots in the 1939–45 War, used many times subsequently for documentary purposes, is of Hitler doing a weird little dance of triumph on hearing the news that France had fallen to the Wehrmacht. Now this, too, turns out to have been a fake, procured by the simple device of removing a few frames from film of Hitler walking. The Führer's tread was unremarkable, but in the camera's version he will dance on through history for ever.

The most horrifying example I know of the camera's power and authority, which will surely be in the history books as an example of the degradation our servitude to it can involve, occurred in Nigeria at the time of the Biafran War. A prisoner was to be executed by a firing squad, and the cameras turned up in force to photograph and film the scene. Just as the command to fire was about to be given, one of the cameramen shouted 'Cut!'; his battery had gone dead, and needed to be replaced. Until this was done, the execution stood suspended. Then, with his battery working again, he shouted 'Action!', and bang, bang, the prisoner fell to the ground, his death duly recorded, to be shown in millions of sitting rooms throughout the so-called civilised world. Some future historian may speculate as to where lay the greatest barbarism, on the part of the viewers, the executioners, or the cameras. I think myself that he would plump for the cameras.

As for the words that accompany the pictures, they have, of course, to be edited down and made to fit, and so are as malleable as the footage, if not more so. There are many authenticated cases of word-faking, like picture-faking. In the case, for instance, of the award-winning television programme *The Selling of the Pentagon*, some of the interviews have been shown to be edited in a way that gives a completely false impression of what was actually said. It goes without saying that none of the awards were withdrawn when the faking was exposed. Nor did the esteem in which the programme was held, diminish. The fraudulence of it apparently did not particularly interest viewers; in their eyes, it just did not matter. Another example of the same sort of fraudulence is Marcel Ophuls's *The Sorrow and the Pity* (*Le Chagrin et la Pitié*), a study of French Resistance in the 1939–45 War, which was shown on BBC 2 and much praised. It happens to be a subject I know quite a lot about because I was a liaison officer with the Gaullist Intelligence set-up, and spent the last year of the war in Paris with them. I can only say, in the light of this experience, that Ophuls's film is distorted and slanted to an almost incredible degree. This, however, as with *The Selling of the Pentagon*, did not prevent it from having an enthusiastic reception. The faking possibilities especially in the cutting room are well-nigh illimitable, and people now clamouring for the televising of Parliament should realise this, and the great power it will put in the hands of whoever edits the footage. He will have to work quickly to get an early screening, which means with little effective supervision, and it will be all too easy for him to make the performance of any MP seem admirable, absurd or contemptible just according to how he puts the footage together.

When I first went to Washington as a newspaper correspondent in 1946, there was a regular White House Press Conference; accredited journalists would gather round the President's desk in the famous Oval Room and ask him questions, which he would answer off-the-cuff. We were not allowed to quote his answers, or to attribute them, but, of course, the procedure was enormously helpful. Then, under President Eisenhower the Press Conference was put on the air, and, with the coming of the Kennedys, lavishly televised. This meant inevitably that the cameramen needed to know in advance who was going to ask questions, because otherwise they couldn't be sure of getting their picture correctly. From this, it is a very small step to start organising the right sort of question. Again, whereas in informal exchanges a President would speak with some frankness, the moment the cameras came they took over, and the whole operation became completely artificial, and ultimately useless, to the point that serious journalists like James Reston never nowadays bother to attend the Press Conference at all. This is assuredly what will happen in Parliament if MP's fall into the trap, and allow their proceedings to be televised. The camera will prove much more effective than Guy Fawkes in destroying Parliament as a deliberative assembly and organ of government.

Faking of the words and pictures to fit the theme has been particularly prevalent in compilation programmes which purport to reconstruct out of stock footage some historical scene or happening. There was the case, for instance, of a programme which celebrated the fiftieth anniversary of the Russian Revolution and used clips taken from Eisenstein's film of the storming of the Winter Palace in Petrograd. This representation of the scene bore little or no relation to what actually occurred, but there it is, on the record. Visually speaking, that is what happened; the footage proves it. The accumulated documentation of our time will be so vast, and for one reason and another, so slanted, that posterity will know nothing about us for sure. The first Dark Ages are lost in the mists of antiquity, with virtually no records; the coming Dark Ages will be equally lost in the blaze of studio lighting, with a superabundance of records, almost all falsified.

In recording contemporary events the camera likewise holds sway. I remember once returning to my hotel in New York and noticing on the way that a crowd had assembled outside what was obviously an embassy or consulate of some sort — I found out afterwards that it belonged to one of the Arab countries. There were the usual students assembled — bra-less girls, bearded men, holding placards with slogans on them; also a police van in attendance, and a number of cops standing by with their truncheons — everything set for a demo. 'What's going on?' I asked, and was told, as though it should have been obvious, that the cameras hadn't yet turned up. I lingered on until they came, and watched them set up and start rolling. Then, 'Action!' whereupon, placards were lifted, slogans shouted, fists clenched; a few demonstrators were arrested and pitched into the police van, and a few cops kicked, until, 'Cut!' Soon the cameras, the cops, and the demonstrators had all departed, leaving the street silent and deserted. Later, in the evening, in my hotel room, I watched the demo on the screen in one of the news programmes. It looked very impressive.

So I suggest that the cameras are our ego's eyes, our age's focus, the repository and emanation of all our fraudulence. Take them to any place of conflict and strife, and hey presto! — in a matter of minutes, trouble stirs for them to register. In his book, called *Do It*, Jerry Rubin, one of the principals in the Chicago conspiracy trial some years ago, has some sage words to say on the subject:

Television creates myths bigger than reality. Whereas a demo drags on for hours and hours, TV packs all the action into two minutes — a commercial for the revolution. On the television screen news is not so much reported as created. An event happens when it goes on TV and becomes myth . . . Television is a non-verbal instrument, so turn off the sound, since no one ever remembers any words that they hear, the mind being a technicolour movie of images, not words. There's no such thing as bad coverage for a demo. It makes no difference what's said: the pictures are the stories.

These observations irresistibly recall to me a remark made in Dostoevsky's uncannily prophetic novel *The Devils*, by the character Peter Verkovensky, who bears a more than passing resemblance to Jerry Rubin and his like. 'A generation or two of debauchery,' Peter Verkovensky exults, 'followed by a little drop of nice fresh blood, just to accustom people, and then the turmoil will begin.' Well, it duly began in Russia, just as Dostoevsky foretold, and seems now to be well under way elsewhere. It would seem to me that the camera may well take its place along with nuclear weaponry and the birth pill as one of the three major apocalyptic portents of our time; the first signifying power in terms of destruction, the second sex in terms of sterility, and the last, actuality in terms of fantasy.

Does this mean that the camera and all its works are wholly evil and incapable of fulfilling God's purposes? Of course not. Everything and everyone ministers to this fulfilment. Even Judas had an essential rôle in the sublime drama of the Passion. God ensures that, whatever we may do in the way of deceiving ourselves, ultimately reality will out. To every fantasy he provides an antidote, just as wherever stinging nettles are, there are also dock leaves to take away the sting. So the camera has to lie, if only to convince us that truth cannot be seen with, but only through the eye, as Blake said. In the same sort of way, we love money; then along comes inflation to reveal money's absurdity; we are obsessed with eroticism, then along comes porn, the *reductio ad absurdum*, or, better perhaps, *ad disgustum*, of sex; we believe in the coming of a kingdom of heaven on earth, and we get the Gulag Archipelago; we crave for facts, and we get computers; we are avid for news, and *Newzak* assails us — news without end, amen.

It is not only to perform his wonders, but also to reveal his ironies that God moves in a mysterious way. It could not possibly be the case that something men have invented, like the media, could never be serviceable to God. If he put into his creatures gifts which enabled them to send words gyrating round the earth and through the stratosphere, then somehow and some time this must serve his purposes. For me personally the media have come to give off a whiff of sulphur, and yet at the end of the day I have to admit that they can enrich as well as debase a life. For instance, once when I was standing waiting for a train in an underground station, a little man — actually, he turned out to be of Greek extraction — came up to me and asked permission to shake my hand. I gladly, and rather absent-mindedly, extended a hand, assuming that he had mistaken me for A. J. P. Taylor, or maybe Mike Yarwood. As we shook hands, he remarked that some words of mine in a radio programme had prevented him from committing suicide. The humbling thing was that I couldn't remember the particular programme he had in mind; doubtless some panel or other, to me buffoonery, and yet a human life had hung on it.

A more ribald example of how incalculable are the consequences of what one does on television was provided by the sequel to a discussion I once had with Archbishop Anthony Bloom on the meaning of pain and affliction. When our session before the cameras was over, for once I felt reasonably satisfied with the exchanges that had taken place between us. The Archbishop is a man of great spirituality, and it seemed to me that we had made a serious, enlightened, and possibly enlightening contribution to a subject that troubles many today. Well, the following morning, when I took a cab at Charing Cross Station, the driver said to me in a jovial, appreciative tone of voice, as though commenting on some particularly neat piece of play in a game of football: 'I saw you last night on the telly with that bloke with a beard; you certainly knocked hell out of him' — an observation which shows once again that in Blakean terms, people look at a television screen with, not through, the eye, and so see on it what they expect, or have been induced to expect, to see.

Then, I have to say that I owe to the media, specifically television, what has proved to be one of the greatest blessings of my life — meeting Mother Teresa. This occurred by chance. I was asked to interview her for BBC television, and on the way to London for the purpose, in the train, looked over some material about her which had been provided. The moment I saw her I realised that, in the words of the prophet Amos, 'the Lord had taken her'. Subsequent acquaintance only confirmed this. She has told me more about our Lord, and helped me to understand more about the Christian faith, far, far more, than anything I have ever read, or thought, or heard on the subject. In the television programme that we made about her, *Something Beautiful for God*, the fact that she does truly live in Christ, and he in her, shines triumphantly through the camera's fraudulence. With God, all things are possible, as Jesus told the disciples when, after he had spoken about rich men and the eye of the needle, they went on to draw the conclusion that there would be no millionaires in heaven. Yes, with God, all things are possible, even bringing the reality of Christ on to the television screen.

We had only five days' filming in Calcutta to make the forty-minute programme on Mother Teresa. The normal allowance for a film of that length would have been two to three months. At every point we had to take all sorts of chances, one of them being to film in the very poor light of her home for the dying, where derelicts from the streets of Calcutta are brought, mostly to die, sometimes to live. To everyone's amazement, including the cameraman, Ken MacMillan's, and mine, this particular footage came out very well, showing the home for the dying, formerly a temple to the Hindu God Khali, bathed in a soft and very beautiful light. There has been some dispute about this. My own feeling was, and remains, that love carried to the point that Mother Teresa has carried it, has its own luminosity, and that the medieval painters who showed saints with halos, were not so wide of the mark as a twentieth-century mind might suppose. In any case, the programme has been shown many times, in many different places, always with great impact.

The moral would seem to be that what is required to make a successful Christian television programme is merely to find a true Christian, and put him or her on the screen. This, rather than any televisual skills or devices, would seem to be the key. Though my own part in making the programme was quite small — just doing the commentary, which meant letting Mother

Teresa speak, and then producing a book about her, which meant holding a pen for her to write — it is a source of great satisfaction and joy to me, and something for which I am truly grateful to the media, that when I meet her Missionaries of Charity, which I quite often do, it usually turns out that a good number of them were drawn into the order by the film or the book.

One of the great attractions of Christianity to me is its sheer absurdity. I love all those crazy sayings in the New Testament — which, incidentally, turn out to be literally true — about how fools and illiterates and children understand what Jesus was talking about better than the wise, the learned and the venerable; about how the poor, not the rich, are blessed, the meek, not the arrogant, inherit the earth, and the pure in heart, not the strong in mind, see God. This is very much in Mother Teresa's vein. Most of what she and her Missionaries of Charity do is, in worldly terms, patently absurd. For instance, salvaging derelicts from the streets, just for them to have the comfort of seeing, even for a few hours or minutes, a loving face, and receiving loving care, rather than closing their eyes on a world implacably hostile, or at best indifferent, whether they lived or died. In purely human terms, such a procedure is clearly ridiculous — so much effort put out for so small a purpose. When the needs of the living are so great, surely, it might be thought, the best thing to do for the dying is just to let them die with perhaps a hypodermic jab to induce forgetfulness and put them to sleep. Mother Teresa sees it differently. When I asked her once what was the difference, in her eyes, between the welfare services and what her Missionaries of Charity do, she said that welfare workers do for an idea, a social purpose, what she and the Missionaries of Charity do for a Person. What we will do for a person is quite different from what we will do as a duty to the society we live in, or in fulfilment of a social idea or ideal. Mothers have starved for their children, wives have trudged for miles and faced appalling dangers when their husbands are in concentration camps to take them food parcels, clean clothes. There is no limit to what love will do, to the point of laying down a life for someone else. Mother Teresa insists that in every single suffering human being she sees the suffering Christ. So a grizzled head, a stricken face laid low in the gutter, is He to whom all care and all love are due. This is more in the nature of a passion than an enlightened purpose. It cannot be taught, but only caught, like a virus, picked up where the saints cherish the poor. Mother Teresa is a notable carrier of infection.

There is something else which I owe to television that has brought me great comfort and joy. Through having a face that, because of television, is liable to be recognised, and being nowadays known as someone who takes a Christian position, people quite often come up to me and, by one means or another, indicate that they, too, are Christians. Thus, when I'm leaving a restaurant, perhaps, a waiter comes padding after me, and silently shakes my hand. Or, in of all crazy places, a make-up room, the girl who is attending to my ancient visage whispers in my ear, 'I love the Lord'. Or turning a corner, I come face to face with a West Indian who, with an enormous grin of recognition, shouts out, 'Dear brother in Christ!' Or an air hostess, stooping to arrange my seat, manages to whisper that she, too, has recently become a Christian. I could go on giving examples for ever.

The experience is altogether delightful, but there is more in it than that. Notice, that it never for a moment occurs to me to want to know whether these diverse people who greet me so charmingly are educated or uneducated, bourgeois or prole- tarian, Roman Catholics or Anglicans or Jehovah's Witnesses, or brown or white or yellow, what their IQ is, how much they earn, or what sort of accent they have. All the different cate- gories we have devised just don't apply. There is but one category: our common fellowship in Christ. This, it seems to me, is a true image of Christian brotherhood. Work-a-day encounters, glorified by participation in a common lot, as children of the same God, redeemed by the same Saviour, destined for the same salvation. Marx saw the apogee of human existence in a victorious proletariat living happily ever after in a society in which government has withered away. Bunyan saw us as souls, for whom, when our pilgrimage is over, the trumpets will sound on the other side. I am for Bunyan.

All through these lectures I have been contrasting the fantasy of the media with the reality of Christ. About the former, the fantasy of the media, I have had much to say — some might contend too much! Let me, then, in conclusion speak about the reality of Christ, and how we may not just recognise it, but live with and by it, making it part of ourselves. Anthony Smith, an old media hand and friend who has been wise enough to take the golden road from Shepherd's Bush to Oxford University, preferring dreaming spires to dreaming aerials, in his excellent book, *The Shadow in the Cave*, uses Plato's famous image of the prisoners in the cage to illustrate the rôle of the media. It is apt indeed.

The prisoners, Socrates explains to Glaucon, are living in a cave which has a wide mouth open towards the light. They are kept in the same place, looking forward only away from the mouth of the cave and unable to turn their heads, for their legs and necks have been fixed in chains from birth. Higher up behind them a fire is burning, and between it and the prisoners there is a road with a low wall built at its side, like the screen over which puppet players put up their puppets. Men walk past under cover of this wall carrying all sorts of things, copies of men and animals, in stone or wood or other material; some of them may be talking and others not.

'It's a strange sort of image,' Glaucon remarks, 'and these are strange prisoners.'

'They're like ourselves,' Socrates replies. 'They see nothing of themselves but their own shadows, or one another's, which the fire throws on the walls of the cave. And so too with the things carried past. If they were able to talk to one another wouldn't they think that the names they used were those of the shadows that went by? And if their prison sent back an echo whenever one of those who went by said a word, what could they do but take it for the voice of the shadow? . . . *The only real thing for them would be the shadows of the puppets.*'

Thus the media world of shadows. In contra-distinction, Christ shows us reality, what life really is, what it is really about, and our true destiny in belonging to it. We escape from the cave, we emerge from the darkness, and instead of shadows we have all around us the glory of God's creation; instead of darkness, light, instead of despair, hope, instead of time and the clocks ticking inexorably on, eternity, which never began and never ends, and yet is sublimely NOW.

What, then, is this reality of Christ, contrasting with all the fantasies whereby men seek to evade it — fantasies of the ego, of the appetites, of power or success, of the mind and the will; valid when first lived and expounded by our Lord himself two thousand years ago, buoying up Western man through all the vicissitudes and uncertainties of Christendom's centuries, and available today, when it is more needed, perhaps, than ever before, as it will be available tomorrow and for ever? It arises simply out of the circumstances that by identifying ourselves with Christ, by absorbing ourselves in his teaching, by living out the drama of his life with him, including especially the Passion — that powerhouse of love and creativity; by living with, by and in him we can be reborn to become new men and women in a new world.

It sounds crazy, as it did to Nicodemus, an early intellectual and potential BBC panelist, who asked how in the world it was possible for someone already born to go back into the womb and be born again. Yet it happens; it has happened innumerable times; it goes on happening. The testimony to this effect is overwhelming. Suddenly caught up in the wonder of God's love flooding the universe, made aware of the stupendous creativity which animates all life, of our own participation in it — every colour brighter, every meaning clearer, every shape more shapely, every note more musical, every word written and spoken more explicit: above all, every human face, all human companionship, all human encounters recognisably a family affair. The animals too, flying, prowling, burrowing, all their diverse cries and grunts and bellowings, and the majestic hill-tops, the gaunt rocks giving their blessed shade, and the rivers faithfully making their ways to the sea — all irradiated with this same new glory in the eyes of the reborn.

What other fulfilment is there that could possibly compare with this? What going to the moon, or exploration of the universe, what victory or defeat, what revolution or counter-revolution, what putting down of the mighty from their seats and exalting of the humble and meek, who then, of course, become mighty in their turn and fit to be put down? A fulfilment that transcends all human fulfilling and yet is accessible to all humans; based on the absolutes of love rather than the relativities of justice, on the universality of brotherhood rather than the particularity of equality, on the perfect service which is freedom rather than on the perfect servitude which purports to be freedom.

Now a last personal word. It so happens that for the past months, here and elsewhere, I have been wholly preoccupied with thinking and talking about this reality of Christ in contra-distinction to the fantasy so evident on every hand in our twentieth-century world. It might seem a little thing, but for me it has been a rather tremendous experience, culminating in being here in this church and speaking these words to you. From what I have said, you know I am convinced that hard and testing days lie ahead; the more so because the prophecy about false shepherds within the fold will be amply fulfilled, indeed, is being fulfilled already. In the nature of things, my own part in these apocalyptic prospects is strictly limited, and I cannot pretend that I wish it were otherwise. How beautiful always is the end of a journey! How exquisite the twilight when a day is ending! How glorious are the closing bars of the *Missa Solemnis*, triumphantly echoing, as they do, all that has gone before! Even so, I felt induced to renew my purpose to serve and live in the reality of Christ, and scribbled down, as it were, my operational orders for such time as remains to me in this world. I venture now to repeat them in case they might be helpful to any who hear or read what I have had to say in these lectures. Here they are:

1. Seek endlessly for God and for his hand in all creation, in the tiniest atom or electron as in the wide expanse of the universe, in our own innermost being as in all fellow-creatures. So, looking, we find him, finding him, we love him, and realise that in every great word ever spoken or written we hear his voice, as in every mean or sordid word we lose it, shutting ourselves off from the glory of his utterance.

2. Live abstemiously. Living otherwise — what Pascal calls 'licking the earth' — imprisons us in a tiny dark dungeon of the ego, and involves us in the pitiless servitude of the senses. So, imprisoned and enslaved, we are cut off from God and from the light of his love.

3. Love and consider all men and women as brothers and sisters, caring for them exactly as we should for Jesus himself if we had the inexpressible honour of ministering to him.

4. Read the Bible and related literature, especially mystical works like the Metaphysical Poets and *The Cloud of Unknowing*. These are the literature of the Kingdom proclaimed in the New Testament; words which became flesh and have dwelt among us, full of grace and truth. Who would live in a new country and not bother to study its literature? I would add here an extra little codicil particularly my own: Love laughter, which sounds loudly as heaven's gates swing open, and dies away as they shut.

Finally:

5. Know Jesus Christ and follow his Way, like Bunyan's Pilgrim, whithersoever it may lead; through pleasant pastures,

over formidable hills, into sloughs and along the Valley of the Shadow of Death itself, but always with the light of the Celestial City, not just in prospect, but *in* one's very eye. Thereby we may learn to live and learn to die.

Thus fortified, we can laugh at the media as Rabelais, in the person of Panurge, laughed at the antics of carnal men; as Cervantes, in the person of Don Quixote, laughed at the antics of crusading men; as Shakespeare, in the person of Sir John Falstaff, laughed at the antics of mortal men.

Nor need we despair to be living at a time when we have lost an Empire on which the sun never set, and acquired a Commonwealth on which it never rises. It is in the breakdown of power that we may discern its true nature, and when power seems strong and firm that we are most liable to be taken in and suppose it can really be used to enhance human freedom and wellbeing, forgetful that Jesus is the prophet of the loser's, not the victor's, camp, and proclaimed that the first will be last, that the weak are the strong, and the fools, the wise. Let us, then, as Christians rejoice that we see around us on every hand the decay of the institutions and instruments of power; intimations of empires falling to pieces, money in total disarray, dictators and parliamentarians alike nonplussed by the confusion and conflicts which encompass them. For it is precisely when every earthly hope has been explored and found wanting, when every possibility of help from earthly sources has been sought and is not forthcoming, when every recourse this world offers, moral as well as material, has been explored to no effect, when in the shivering cold the last faggot has been thrown on the fire and in the gathering darkness every glimmer of light has finally flickered out — it is then that Christ's hand reaches out, sure and firm, that Christ's words bring their inexpressible comfort, that his light shines brightest, abolishing the darkness for ever. So, *finding in everything only deception and nothingness, the soul is constrained to have recourse to God himself and to rest content with him.*

For the author's replies to questions posed by those attending this lecture, please turn to page 98.

QUESTIONS

QUESTIONS FOLLOWING
THE FIRST LECTURE

Q. *How do you reconcile your own appearance on television with what you say about it? Surely as Christians we are meant to be putting some constructive ideas into television and radio.*

A. My own appearance on television is merely the same as my own appearance in any magazine or newspaper or whatever it might be, in which I have functioned as a communicator. In other words, television is a method of communication, and when an opportunity has arisen to avail myself of it, I've done so. But if you say, 'put something constructive into it', of course, in so far as one takes part in it, one does one's poor best to use it in that way. What I was trying to indicate, using an imaginary fourth temptation to which our Lord was subjected, was really that this medium, *by its nature*, doesn't lend itself to constructive purposes.

Sir Charles Curran was very insistent on the point that I'd mentioned no specific programmes, but I couldn't see any reason to mention programmes. I've taken part in many, and I think I know as well as anybody how they are produced. I was trying to think in terms, not of the effect of this or that programme, but of the effect of the medium itself on people; the part it is playing in our lives, but specifically in our lives as Christians.

Q. *Do you not think that the content of television, and the fantasy and so forth that you've been talking about, is in fact a reflection of a fairly corrupt society, and as a Christian do you not think that, rather than simply decrying television as a medium, you should be trying to put more into it, and change its content?*

A. Of course, I entirely agree that what I was criticising or drawing attention to in television reflects what is going on in our society. In the same sort of way, St. Paul, in his Epistle to the Corinthians, told the Christians in Corinth that the society they were living in was not compatible with their Christian faith, which was clearly the case. He did not, however, go on to tell them that they must participate in the Corinthian way of life; for instance, get a job as a gladiator, and try to show that there can be Christian gladiators. It is a fallacy of our time that we can usefully participate in whatever exists. In point of fact, very often in history, what exists is antipathetic to what, as Christians, we believe. If you want to know my absolutely candid opinion, I think the best thing to do is not to look at television, and to that end, I have, as has been said, disposed of my set. But that is just my personal opinion. What I'm saying is that we have created a medium which, by its nature, trafficks in fantasy, and I have tried to show, very inadequately, that the fantasy extends to what is called news, which is the medium's basic commodity. This is not the fault of the people who direct and operate the television networks. They have got an appalling job on their hands, because, whatever they may do, what comes out on the screen is fantasy rather than reality. I think it is important that Christians should recognise this, and that they should realise what it is doing to people, in every field, including especially the one in which it might be supposed factual objectivity was most insisted upon, namely, in the projection of news — the biggest fantasy and delusion of all.

Q. *What influence, if any, do you think that a Christian can have by being involved in the media, and I don't just mean television?*

A. I'm glad you make the point about not meaning just television. The media, as I try to stress in these lectures, includes journalism in all its aspects as well as television. What a Christian can do in whatever part of the media he may be working, wherever his lot may be cast, is to continue to be a Christian. Thereby, he may not be able to change the media appreciably; they have their own conditions and circumstances. Inside the media, however, he can and should sustain his Christian witness. He may find this very hard, very hard indeed, because of the incompatibility between God and Mammon—in this case, between Christ and the media. We are told to make our light shine before men. That is our Christian duty; the results are God's concern, not ours.

Q. *I speak as one with a high regard for media men, and I'm thinking of people like Matthew, Mark, Luke and John, from whom we have gained a lot, and I wonder whether you would like to comment on whether the real danger with television isn't in the sheer quantity of the stuff.*

A. I entirely agree with that. I've often said that if, by some misfortune, I became dictator, my first decree would be that there would be television only from seven to ten every evening. I think that what you say is true, that it is utterly impossible to fill the screen with worthwhile material for the enormous number of hours during which it now has to be filled. To me, it is a terrible fact that the average citizen spends some eight years of his life looking into a television screen. None the less, it's a fact which has to be faced, and the implications of it have to be faced. Not in the sense of merely pointing the finger at those responsible for filling the television screen, or in the sense of persuading ourselves that nonetheless, despite appearances to the contrary, what it has to show us is beneficial.

Q. *In the temptations, Christ didn't say that bread was evil, he didn't say it was useless. He saw it in a perspective that was much wider, and in that perspective he saw it as having a positive use. From all you've been saying, I'm not convinced that you are presenting your fourth temptation in the way that Christ might have seen it. In his perspective, the media might be seen as having a positive use in today's world.*

A. I should be very interested, if you ever have time to work it out, to know the basis on which you think our Lord would accept the Devil's offer of prime time on television. I can't see him accepting it myself. I thought a lot about it when I was preparing these lectures, and it seemed to me quite certain that he would have rejected this fourth offer as surely as he did the other three. The manner in which his teaching spread through the world, following on St. Paul's amazing missionary journeys, was surely the way he wanted it to be propagated, and I don't feel that television would have fitted in with that way. It's an arguable point, I agree. Of course we have to make use of the means of communication which exist. But we also have this other duty, which is a prime duty for Christians, to make our light shine before men, and it's not always easy to know just how this may best be done.

Q. *I'm not, I think, greatly interested as to whether Jesus of Nazareth would have accepted television appearance had TV been available at the time. What I am interested in is whether the living Christ, who is incarnate today through the members of his body, is to be seen and heard and discovered through the media. It seems to me that what you are saying implies that you would consider, for example, Mother Teresa to have been wrong to have taken part in that interview with you some years ago.*

A. With God all things are possible, and Mother Teresa's appearance on television was supremely useful and successful because, for once, the total dedication of her life broke through the fantasy-proneness of the medium. Not for a moment am I saying that there are no special cases. I'm trying to give my views on the nature of television as such; on the nature of its influence, the relation of its fantasy to the reality of Christ, and on the enormous chasm that lies between these two. I agree that it's a chasm which can, in very special circumstances, be bridged. If I sounded as though I was dogmatically suggesting that there was no possibility at all, that is not so. But the chasm exists, and is growing ever wider, and the viewers in their millions are all on the fantasy side.

Q. *I'd like to ask, what is the basic ethos of the BBC? What standards do they have there? If they are not Christian, do they have standards which govern their selection of programmes? Or is it a free-for-all? As society becomes more degenerate, will television automatically become more degenerate along with it? Or do they have in the last resort absolute standards beyond which they will not go?*

A. I think that's an absolutely first-rate question. It is, in fact, *the* question. I believe myself — but of course, I could be completely wrong — I firmly believe myself, that one of the difficulties that people like Charles Curran are confronted with in their very difficult jobs is that, when once they depart from Christian values, there *are* no alternative ones. Theoretically there are, but in practice there aren't. That's why I brought in Reith because he was the man — perhaps the very last media boss — who desperately, even crazily, tried to hold on to Christian guidelines. But once they cease to be acceptable there is not an agreeable set of alternative ones — humanistic ones or what you will — there is in fact none. That is why in my opinion — and I fancy Charles might agree with me here — by and large, the standard is falling all the time.

Sir Charles Curran:

Let me just say one or two words. I don't know whether you were trying to provoke me, Malcolm. My life is not a penance. My life is a proud one. I'm proud of what we do, like Jimmy Carter. I don't spend my life agonising about why I'm in the wrong place. I worry about how to do the right thing in the place that I am.

The question here is very relevant. Are there any standards beyond which the BBC won't go? It's a funny way to put it, because I'm interested in freedom, not in taboos. I don't believe that most people in this country share my dogmatic beliefs, and you know that I could prove that almost automatically in the census. There is no common body of accepted dogma. Therefore there are no principles which are universally accepted — not even, Malcolm, Christian principles. What I have to do, therefore, if I haven't got an agreed dogmatic basis — and there hasn't been one in Europe since the Reformation, and in the world for much longer — if there isn't an agreed dogmatic basis, I have to look for a pragmatic basis on which we can proceed. And the only pragmatic basis that answers, rests on the acceptance, or otherwise, of what you do. It is the practical facts of behaviour which decide what you can do. It may not be a very exalted creed, but it is the only one you can live by, if you are trying to offer things to people with different dogmatic bases and sometimes with no dogmatic basis at all. What you cannot do, under any circumstances — and I don't care what creed you follow — what you cannot do is say, 'My will is superior to yours, and it enables me to use the instrument which you gave me in order to impose something on you'. There is a sacredness of human personality which I am not entitled, as a servant, to invade. That's my fundamental belief, and that's my answer to your question.

Q. *May I ask Sir Charles, please, to make a few comments. Cyril Bennett killed himself last week, or the week before. He was in a similar position, I believe, to yours, albeit on a somewhat lower level, and engaged in trying to please all of the people all of the time. According to* The Sunday Times, *this is in fact what eventually broke the man. He found himself to be down in the ratings, and the situation, as you have said, was that he was not able to impose his personality upon the medium. I should like to hear from you also whether in fact this is not the whole basis of the trouble with television — that someone does have to choose what to put on, and here we ought to be quite specific about our evaluation of programmes — programmes, I say, such as* The Generation Game, Mr. & Mrs., *or four hours of sport each Saturday. These programmes are screened purely because they are what people want, not because there is anything particularly edifying in them, or that they are in any way what you yourself would regard as worthwhile. I think this is probably the basis of the tension within the industry and perhaps within your job as well — that you have to provide programmes that people want, and yet try to keep to a standard. Therefore, I was wondering if you would like to put television in a league table with other media such as the theatre, cinema and so on.*

Sir Charles Curran:

I'm not quite sure what the significance of that is. No, I wouldn't — that's a very simple answer. On Cyril Bennett — all men and women, and especially women, have their trials, and some of them cannot face them, and when they can't, the only thing you should say, even if they're Jewish, is: 'God have mercy on their souls'. That's the only thing you should say. As to the reports in the press — it is just not true that he got into this state of mind because of the ratings. He may have been under stress: we all are, in this business. So far as I can see, this was a classic case of what the doctors call double stress. Trouble at home, and very strong stresses at work. And I think it is quite wrong to think that a man as talented as Cyril Bennett would have gone under to something which was entirely a matter of his professional life. Now as to *The Generation Game* — I enjoy it very much, it is worthwhile for me because it is a relaxation, as it is to many other people, and there is nothing corrupting about it that I can see. I also enjoy sport. I interrupt my reading of my BBC papers on Sunday, which I do all day, for one hour on Sunday afternoon in order to watch *Rugby Special*, and nothing will divert me from that, because, once again, this is relaxation, and there is also the technical interest in the game. I can see nothing wrong in that. I don't like to use the word 'puritan' in a perjorative sense, but you, I suspect, are a 'Puritan'.

Q. *Can I just put my question very quickly? Simply to ask whether you would make a distinction between Christ appearing live on television and his being edited. We've just had an example of that from Sir Charles, who tells us that the media reports were inaccurate, and he has told us what he believes to be the truth. A lot of us suffer from that; there was the case recently of two programmes put out about the Church of England which gave a completely false impression because of the way they were edited. I wonder if you would make a distinction — that Christ would have appeared live, but he wouldn't have agreed to appear in an edited version.*

A. It is, of course, substantially true, that the editor wields enormous power, and this can be, and often is, used to distort and slant what has been recorded on film or video tape. I do not, however, think myself that the prospect of a live appearance would have induced our Lord to succumb to the fourth temptation. I think he would have declined in all circumstances, actually, and I think he would have been right. The wonder, you see, of the Word which becomes flesh, and dwells among us cannot get on to film, cannot get on to video, cannot get into a camera, Mother Teresa notwithstanding. In the beginning was the *Word*, and the Word became flesh, not celluloid.

QUESTIONS FOLLOWING
THE SECOND LECTURE

Q. *I haven't read any of your books, but when were you actually converted, and when did you actually accept Christ as your Saviour? I have been reading since your lecture last Monday some of your writings in the earlier editions of* Punch, *and I can see no exhortation in your* Punch *writings for the media to propagate the Gospel via the printed word or by vision.*

A. That's a question I can easily answer in the sense that there was no point in my life when I underwent any dramatic change. I would say that for me at any rate, the process has been not a sudden Damascus road experience, but more like the journeying of Bunyan's Pilgrim, who constantly lost his way, fell into sloughs, was locked up in Doubting Castle and terrified out of his wits in the Valley of the Shadow of Death, but still, through it all had a sense of moving towards light, moving out of time towards eternity. That's the most that I can claim. As for my earlier writings — I don't consider that my contributions to *Punch* (most of which, by the way, were anonymous), provide a fair specimen.

Q. *I would like to ask you, as I've listened to your lectures, your view of the media: including everything, from Bronowski's* Ascent of Man *to the murky depths of* Family. *You seem to project this view — that the media are totally spurious, utterly, hopelessly useless, and that truth, or God, cannot in any way come through the media. Sir Charles Curran last week called you a Manichean, and it seems to me that you are, for surely the teaching of the Incarnation is that through the Incarnation God can enter into every aspect of man's experience and world. But you are saying that he can't, that here is an aspect of man's world that God can't enter.*

A. I get your point perfectly. I shouldn't say at all that the media are beyond God's reach, and cannot convey truth, but I would say that they are, by their nature, primarily dedicated to fantasy, and that their effect on people is to enclose them in fantasy. That's why I imagined that our Lord would have turned down a fourth temptation to appear on television in prime time for the same reason that he turned the other three down — because it would have involved him in the apparatus of power — time, money, all that sort of thing. What I've tried to do in these lectures is to show that there is a gulf between reality, which for Christians is Christ, and the world of fantasy that the media project, and that Western people are being enormously misled by being induced to regard things on the screen as real, when actually they are fantasy. But, of course, God can use all things — even television, even you and me.

Q. *Your arguments, it seems to me, are built largely around analogies, and I'd like to suggest at this point that some of your analogies are inappropriate, and on two I will take you up. First, I'd suggest it is a legacy of the moral rectitide of the nineteenth century that has given us the thorough-going capitalist faith in consumerism and individualism, whereas faith in the revolution of Christ is the forefront of the call to responsibility towards the underprivileged non-consumers. Secondly, you mystify me in that your objection to consensus is phrased in such a way as to define consensus as anything that dares to diverge from the previously held consensus.*

A. First I'd like to explain that whatever strictures I may direct against the world now, it doesn't mean that I think that what was going on in the world a hundred years ago was good. That implication is not there. I think that human beings are always governed badly, and as far as their worldly pursuits are concerned, I agree with Pascal, that these are diversions from the true purpose in life, which is to look for God. If you make Christ a revolutionary, then you associate him with power, and there is nothing that I can find in the Gospels, that has ever been attributed to him, or that any of the Christian mystics have ever conveyed, which conceivably suggests that his Kingdom could be brought to pass through the exercise of power. So there you and I are in disagreement. But I see your point, and I should not like you to think that, because certain current trends are to be abhorrent, I believe there was a golden age in the past — not at all. After all, the Christian faith was spread in Europe by St. Paul in the reign of the Emperor Nero — not an exemplary ruler; indeed, one who makes even some of ours seem quite reasonably enlightened by comparison.

With regard to the question of consensus, my objection to it is not that it differs from yesterday's version, but that it is collective thought, and I distrust and fear that. There is something, to me, very sinister about this emergence of a weird kind of conformity, or orthodoxy, particularly among the people who operate the media, so that you can tell in advance exactly what they will say and think about anything. It is true that so far they have not got an Inquisition to enforce their orthodoxy. but they do have ways of enforcing it which make the old thumbscrews and racks seem quite paltry.

Q. *As far as we know, Jesus never wrote anything for our consumption. Do you think that this confirms your idea of the impotence of the media images, and have you any other comments on this fact?*

A. Jesus certainly didn't write anything, and I think it's quite likely that he didn't know how to write, which to me is an enormous enhancement of the story. I don't think, however, that his not writing anything has any particular bearing on the question of images. The Christian faith has come to us in words, not images; I find that passage in the first chapter of the Gospel according to St. John — the Word becoming flesh, and dwelling among us full of grace and truth — one of the most beautiful and profound things ever written. If it had come to us in images instead of words, it would not have lived as it has.

Q. *My name is John Lang, and I'm Head of Religious Broadcasting at the BBC. You know me by sight, I think, though last time we met you mistook me for a Conservative Member of Parliament who had lost his seat* (M. — But that was a compliment: if I mistook you for a Conservative Member of Parliament who had won his seat, then you'd have a complaint to make!) *I'd just like to refer briefly to what you said about consensus of opinion among my colleagues. I'd like to say very humbly that I don't think you know very many of them. It is true that until 1971, perhaps the beginning of 1972, you worked closely with some of them in television, but the department is quite large, and the opinions held within it are very varied. It seems to me that in speaking in the way you have done, you are in fact guilty of a slur. I regret it, because I don't think that your observation is based on knowledge. I can't speak of your knowledge over a wider field, but I can over the field which I know well.*

A. Would I be permitted to ask you a question? Do you think that when I suggested, for instance, that a Roman Catholic priest who whole-heartedly believed in *Humanae Vitae* would be unlikely to be comfortable in a religious broadcasting organisation — do you think that would be true or not?

Q. *There is such a priest in the department . . . and you would find*

many people who believe that the Ten Commandments were some-thing never to be gainsaid, were God's voice to man, not in a merely historic sense but for ever.
A. Well, that's good news.

Q. *The point I want to put to you is this. We gain tremendous insights through the Incarnation — the vulnerability of God, the unconditional love that induces him to risk taking upon himself the nature and being of our fallen humanity. I wonder if you have a word of encouragement, because it has not yet come across, for those who in the name of Christ have likewise taken the risk of working in the media you describe so negatively.*
A. I have the utmost respect for them, which I have frequently expressed. I don't want to say that Christians shouldn't work in the media, but I think they are working against something rather than with something in so doing, because of the media's propensity to fantasy. That was the point that I was trying to make, but I would certainly rejoice to think that a Christian like you should be working in the media, as I rejoice to hear what the Head of BBC Religious Broadcasting has told me, that there are priests on his staff who really, whole-heartedly believe in *Humanae Vitae*, as I do myself, and that he has colleagues who are not prepared to bypass the Ten Commandments.

Q. *A propos this notion of consensus, could you say a word as to why we do not have on television or radio minority groups like Jehovah's Witnesses, Mormons, Seventh Day Adventists, and other people of that nature? It seems to me there is a consensus on television that excludes these people from presenting their views. I wonder if you would say something to that.*
A. I'm afraid you really have to direct that question to Mr. Lang or Sir Charles. I have no hand in such matters at all. That there *is* a consensus, I have no doubt whatsoever. It is my opinion that our society is somehow generating this consensus,

and that the media, often unconsciously, adjust themselves to it. That is my impression.

Q. *I'm a little confused by your setting image over against word, as if image were bad and words were good. Certainly the Bible has a lot to say about words, and about the Word of God, but I think that image in the Bible isn't just a negative term, and that Christ himself is described as God's Image, and not God's Word. I'm interested to hear that you haven't taken down your antennae for radio.*

A. In fact, you don't have to have antennae for radio and what's more, you don't have to buy a licence for it! It has that enormous advantage, though you do, it's true, sometimes find yourself listening to things you might not want to hear. The image in the sense that I've been using it is the one referred to in the Second Commandment — the image men make and then worship. I think it's a different use of the word, if you'll allow me to say so, from men made in the image of God.

Q. *Where do you draw the line between the right use of images and the wrong use?*

A. The image, of course, that the camera makes is not to be equated with the image that an artist makes; and the key to this whole question of the media, so far as the visual part of it is concerned, is the camera. If men made an image in the sense of a painting, say Blake's paintings, which I greatly admire — they are expressions in colour and shape of their sense of reality. I can't equate that with what a camera does. When we talk of images in connection with the media we are talking about camera images.

Sir Michael Swann:

Mr. Muggeridge, it seems to me that I should try to reply on behalf of the BBC because you have been clobbering us, even if our Head of Religious Broadcasting has answered you back handsomely. I want, if I may, very briefly to reminisce. You will remember the last occasion when I heard you talking in a church — St. Giles Cathedral in Edinburgh — at that time you were the student-elected Rector of that ancient University and I was its Vice-Chancellor. You got up in the pulpit and you denounced the student body in a big way for all the sins of the flesh, pot, pills and the lot; you then resigned as Rector, and a splendid and dramatic occasion it was.

Some five years later, I moved to the BBC and once again I find myself in a church, with you thumping my organisation. If I wasn't of a rather phlegmatic nature, I'd feel paranoid perhaps. I did then think that you listened to the noisy, extremist students, and you didn't listen to the quieter ones who were good people but didn't make quite so much noise. You no doubt felt, and I think you said so at the time, that they should stand up and be counted.

I have a feeling that you're making the same mistake over broadcasting and the media. You are latching on to a few faults, perhaps numerous faults, but you are ignoring a great many good people who do a great many good things. I believe you ought to have those aerials re-installed and be made to listen and watch a little more than you do: I think John Lang is right, and you are wrong.

A. If you'll forgive me for saying so, I don't think that the difference with Mr. Lang was anything that aerials could correct: I was simply (according to his reckoning) misinformed about his present staff.

I'm fascinated by your recollection of the circumstances in which I resigned the rectorship of Edinburgh University, and, of course, I don't want to revive that old controversy. It does, however, seem to me an extraordinary thing to say, when the student newspaper, and every expression of student opinion, was freely and rather venomously directed against me, that I failed to observe that this was a tiny minority. If most people were on my side, they kept very quiet about it. The same thing would go for quite a number of members of the staff as well.

In this business of television I am simply tremendously conscious that the medium is doing something to a Christian society which is dangerously destructive. Not deliberately, I don't believe that for a moment! I believe that Mr. Lang and his colleagues are good men. All the same, I consider that with their connivance something terrible is being done, and I express this in terms of fantasy and reality, which is admittedly an over-simplification. Working in television, as I have, over a long period of time, I've seen it grow, I've watched how it's operated, and the effect it has on people; on their values, how they look at life, and I see it as a grave danger. The only answer that I can find is the Christian answer. I don't think there's any humanist or rationalist answer. But I don't see you, Michael, or Charles Curran, or Brian here, as diabolical figures: in a way it would be much easier if you were. But I think you have in your hands something which is, I repeat, in process of destroying the moral and spiritual basis of our way of life. Take just the showing of old films. Try as I will, I cannot understand how anyone could want to put a film like *Rosemary's Baby* into people's sitting rooms. I don't know how they can manage to bring themselves to do it. And they're doing it, and they're going to do it with still more horrible films now in the pipeline. Nor can I imagine how they persuade themselves that arrangements for late-evening viewing and so on really work, in the sense of preventing children from seeing programmes liable to harm them, because everybody knows they don't.

Notice we've talked a great deal about television, but most of my life has been spent in working for newspapers and magazines, and the situation there is even clearer. I think that we shall come to have to reckon with it, to face it, and probably, since I take a very pessimistic view of how that reckoning will work out, it will involve, not just my having my aerials removed, but actually, along with others who see all this, deciding to detach ourselves from the media altogether. Well, I should suppose the early Christians in Corinth kept away from the games.

QUESTIONS FOLLOWING THE THIRD LECTURE

Q. *You seem to me this evening to have come full circle, in saying that the media can present the truth about Christ, if only by a miracle. Cannot we say this about all communication, whether it is between one person and the next, whether it is by means of preaching or lecture, or by anything that is written down? Isn't it a miracle each time that this truth is truly communicated? We have to get our scale of priorities right and recognise that the more technology we put into communication, the more difficult it is for truth to get through. One could have a rating of, say, person to person communication, lecturing, and go down the scale. From the things you've said to us you would obviously put television at the bottom of that scale. Still, the fact is that, where God is truly communicated, it remains a miracle.*

A. I would agree with that entirely, and only disagree when you say that I've gone full circle. What I've tried to show is precisely what you yourself have said — that technology itself, including the camera, has enormously interfered with this communication between men, distorted it, deflected it, making it, on the one hand, from the Devil's point of view, advantageous in that it facilitates deception, and on the other, making it the more difficult to communicate those things that are true and real. The miracle of our existence is that we should be able, however inadequately, by words or by whatever other means, to convey to our fellow men something of what we've seen and looked at and learned about the great transcendental truths of our existence. I agree there absolutely. But please remember that today I have a most sympathetic Chairman, whereas on the other two occasions I had the media brass here, and it is their terrible complacency, their terrible belief that because they can reach millions of people, therefore what is said will be a million times more effective, that I find so shocking. The bromides they hand out so lavishly are full of poison; that's what I've been trying to draw attention to.

It's a most marvellous thing, as I said in the first lecture, that we have this reality in Christ to live with and in, because of the brilliance as a communicator of the Apostle Paul, because of the brilliance as communicators of the men who wrote the Gospels, because of the brilliant communication achieved by all the art, literature, philosophy, all the stupendous creativity of one sort or another derived from the sublime drama of the New Testament. Then we come to the media, ever seeking, by whatever means, to reach more and more people, and the danger arises of their becoming a vicious, corrupting influence, wholly outweighing any possible advantages in the way of speed and transmission that they may offer. What I am saying is that it might be necessary, in such a case, for Christians to decide what they are going to do about it, as it was necessary for the Christians in Corinth to decide what they were going to do about the games in the corrupt, depraved society in which they were living.

Q. *Given what you were saying tonight, that the camera can show forth the reality of Christ ... I, myself, being a Christian, am returning to the States to enter journalism school and hopefully photo-journalism. How can I, as a Christian best do this? What are some guidelines you could give me? Or some absolute limits that you could set for me? How can I use photo-journalism in the States to show forth the reality of Christ?*

A. I don't think there are any rules for that, at all. I think you will find yourself having unexpected difficulties, not for personal reasons, nor because of your colleagues, but because of the camera itself, because of what's required of the camera. Supposing there'd been a roving cameraman in Jerusalem at the time of the Crucifixion, I doubt if he'd have been up on Golgotha filming there. The values on a basis of which he would be operating wouldn't take in that scene. All the same, we have to remember that with God all things are possible. So I say to you that if you, as a Christian, are staunch, true to the reality of Christ, and never allow it to be lost to view, then whatever you try to do will be serving him. That's all one can say. There's no rule.

Q. *This is more of a witness, really than a question. For a long time I've felt that I had almost lost my faith, in fact I would say that I had so little that it was practically non-existent, and about a month ago I made a recommitment. Several things that you've said have struck home really deeply to me: for instance, when you said in your first lecture that practically everything that happened in your life became a little miracle from God. That's been happening to me in the past month, in that I've walked into amazing conversations and situations in all my work places, and I feel that God has given me such confirmation of true reality. A lot of what you've said, especially last week about lashing yourself to the mast, and going on, has meant so much to me that I wanted to say thank you.*

A. You couldn't say anything nicer. You couldn't say anything that would make me happier to have been at this podium. I say God bless you.

Q. *If we see something on television that we do not like, what do you suggest that we do? What is the most effective way to combat this?*

A. It's a very difficult question, to which I have given a good deal of thought, especially when I was chairman of the broad-casting section of Lord Longford's Pornography Report. If you write and complain, it's extremely improbable that anything will be done about it — there's a special department, from long experience highly skilled in neutralising complaints. If you publicly protest, you may, alas, be helping the very thing you're protesting about, because it's very unlikely that it will be stopped, and there's nothing that the producers of objectionable TV programmes, films, plays and books, like better than to have protests. I, myself, have heard in a television studio, the hope expressed that with a bit of luck, what is being put on the screen will get a blast from Mrs. Whitehouse. I must in honesty say to you that I think the time will come, and perhaps has come, when Christians will simply not have television, because of the large and growing admixture of what is really evil in it. Obviously this will be particularly the case if you have children in your household. As I have already said, it is the most disgusting hypocrisy to claim that by timing a programme, or by issuing special warnings about it, young people can be prevented from seeing it.

Q. *Mr. Muggeridge, you've obviously been spending some time cogitating on your life, and I'm wondering if, if you had the opportunity, you would live it over again the same, and if not, what would you change?*
A. Theoretically, one ought to be able to say: 'All the awful things I've done, I wish I hadn't done.' But actually it wouldn't be true. I've been writing my autobiography, and this forces you to examine your life with some closeness. As I've pro-ceeded with this examination, I've come to see my life, in its tiny way, as part of the whole drama of creation, enacted by creatures made in the image of God, living in time, capable of conceiving perfection but by their nature imperfect. If, there-fore, I were to say that I wish I hadn't done this or that, it would amount to wishing that my life, in its totality, had been

other than it has been, and that I hadn't been vouchsafed such glimpses of truth through living it that I have been vouchsafed. It's a slightly complicated point, really. If you were to have said to Shakespeare when he was writing *King Lear*: 'Why do you make that poor old king suffer like that? Why don't you give him a sedative at the end of Act I?' Shakespeare's answer would have been: 'Well, I quite see your point, and I'm also sorry for the old boy, but if he were to be given a sedative at the end of Act I, there would be no play.' When we offer our lives to God it is in their totality, not revised for his inspection. I shudder to think it must be so, but so it is.

Q. *I was going to ask you when you started off, to do a hatchet job on one of your own films — how you've faked it all — but I think you've shown us that truth can break through. I should like to add, I think, that it's the purity of motive of the people who are doing it that is important. That's what I'd like to say to our American friend: I think that a Christian with pure motives can be used by Christ. It seems to me that St. Paul went to Rome because it was the centre of power of the world of his day, a fulcrum whereby he could get Christian ideas to the whole empire, to the known world, quickly, and I don't see how Christians can get Christian ideas to the whole world without using the media, and without many more Christians militantly going into the media and using the media to take Christianity to millions of people around the world.*

A. I take your point absolutely. Of course, first of all I entirely agree that Christians who work in the business of communications must work in them as Christians. This is clear. With regard to St. Paul going to Rome, historically he was taken to Rome as a prisoner. He didn't book a ticket on the Pan-Am. He was glad to go there, and proposed going on to Spain; he was a traveller, an envoy of our Lord.

With regard to the millions of people, I'm not so sure. I considered it in my first lecture in connection with the fourth temptation: whether our Lord would have accepted a spot at prime time on Rome Television by courtesy of Lucifer, Inc. You see, this business of communication is very mysterious; after fifty years at it, it remains enormously mysterious. Drop a word, some quite casual word, and it has an impact; mount an elaborate operation, with masses of people and speeches reaching far and wide, and nobody notices. Let me give a simple example taken from secular matters. I'm quite sure that, say, Orwell's *Animal Farm* has done much more damage to Communism than all the activities of the Voice of America, the Overseas Service of the BBC, Radio Free Europe, the whole lot put together. I was delighted to hear the other day that it got into Poland on the quota of farming books!

So I'm always very dubious about estimating influence by counting heads. God speaks to us in a still, small voice, and leaves the thunderous words to Caesar. The truth is that what is effective is truth. I suppose that if you'd seen St. Paul landing in Europe, and someone had said: 'Do you think *that* man is going to be the founder and inspirer of a civilisation that will last for two thousand years?' you would have said: 'No, he's a poor guy; he ought to have somebody with power and influence to back him'. He had, of course, but not of this world. These things are very mysterious.

Q. *I hope that you won't close these super lectures by having us all throw out our television sets, or indeed asking that there should be no Christians involved in all the arts and media communications. For surely too long, Christians have been on the touchline watching the game, and not involved in it. It is tough, and it is difficult, but some surely must be there, making it and working at it. Wasn't it the artists in the Book of Exodus who were the first people, under the ordination of God, to receive God's blessing and the gift of the Holy Spirit? So a small group of us are struggling.*

A. I know you are, and nobody could admire what you're doing more than I do. I think it's a marvellous thing, and I am sure that such endeavour is amply justified and necessary, and I applaud what you're doing with all my heart. But this business of involvement also has its dangers. Too heavy a price can be paid for involvement. Again, I don't think there's any rule of thumb that one can fall back on.

Q. *'Don't put your daughter on the stage, Mrs. Worthington', is still in the minds of many people here today; when their daughter has been given a gift, a talent, and indeed she comes along and says, 'Why shouldn't I? Can I not be a Christian, and a dancer?' Can she not be a Christian, and a dancer?*
A. Oh yes, absolutely, but I just think you mustn't err the other way either. I have a great sympathy with the Puritans in shutting down the theatre, given the social circumstances when they did it. Obviously no Christian should divorce himself from the world he's living in. But again, thinking of St. Paul, supposing some young Christian convert had come up and said: 'I've just been offered a marvellous job as a gladiator, and do you think a Christian gladiator would be a good idea?' I suspect that that dear good man would have said, 'No, I think not'. It depends entirely on the circumstances of the case. One of the many reasons that I so abominate the present mania for erotic and pornographic art and entertainment is because of the unfortunate people who professionally have to take part in it. If art becomes decadent beyond a certain point, I'm sure that you wouldn't wish to seem to lend it your approval.

Q. *Am I right in thinking that George Orwell wrote* Animal Farm *while working next door? At the BBC?* (M. — Yes.) *I'm amazed not to have heard a stinging rebuke from you about all the appalling noise with which these fantasies are hurled at us. If there was any method of control of this noise by the DOE, the manufacturers of commercial TV sets and broadcasting authorities, perhaps there could be co-existence with television. As you're no longer a televiewer, I'd like to tell you something of what you're missing: it's*

*possible to go across the Mexican desert with Geoffrey Boswall,
enjoy submarine life from your armchair, a great condor sweeping
over the Andes.*
A. I shall burst into tears in a moment.

Q. *I implore you to take back one small aerial, a BBC one.*
A. No, no, I shall never take it back, though it's very kind of
you to suggest it. Your point about Orwell is an interesting one.
He told me something that I never tire of laughing at and
repeating whenever a good opportunity occurs — when he was
devising the Ministry of Truth in *1984*, the BBC was his model.
He worked there in the war, and his Ministry of Truth bears
unmistakable traces of this experience — all those long, chilly
corridors are unmistakably Broadcasting House. Over the
question of noise, of course, it is an appalling thing; something
that among many other factors is gradually driving people mad.
I'm not in any way tolerant of it myself. You've said that you
can enjoy the Andes sitting in your armchair; but that is
precisely one of the reasons I've had my aerials removed,
because I don't want to enjoy the Andes sitting in my armchair.

Q. *Speaking as a person who works in television, may I try in a
final sally to get your shaft against television removed to the
broader sense of the media? In your points about truth being
reported on television, I was interested, in your first lecture, to note
that your examples came from your journalistic days, when you sat
in Cairo and imagined what was happening, for us back home. Do
you not think that if it was, say, four hundred years ago, about the
time of the invention of the printing press, you would be having your
spectacles removed, because you would be giving us exactly the same
lecture. Isn't it a terrible thing if we are going to receive all this
subjective opinion in the written word, and believe it to be true?*
A. That's well put, and perhaps I should have dealt with the
matter you raise. I don't myself in any way equate the invention
of printing with the invention of television. There are enormous

differences between the two, and one of the most obvious ones
is that the printed word — which I hold in veneration — is not
subject to the same centralised control as television. In other
words, many people can print clandestinely and openly, with
flat-bed presses or with rotaries, and so on: but in the case of
television, you have to have, by the nature of the technology, a
centralised control. What has not been worked out is whose
control, or in what terms that control is to be exercised.

Words, printed words, are words that have arisen in a human
mind. They are connected with thought and with art. But
photography or filming, is a completely different thing. It is
machine made; as I said in my third lecture today, it is seeing
with, not through, the eye; looking but not seeing.

Q. *It is possible to both lie and tell the truth in both media; with
both photography and words. Surely what you are saying is that
it's easier in visuals.*
A. It's very nearly impossible to tell the truth in television, but
you can try very hard. As far as the word is concerned, spoken
or written, it has been used, and continues to be used, for
purposes of deception, and for evil purposes like pornography.
This is absolutely true. But, you see, a word comes from a man.
Putting it in its simplest terms, if I write a novel, signed by my
name, I am saying these are my thoughts, these are my views,
these are my impressions, and the response of the reader is
according. If you set up a camera and take a film, that is not
considered to be anybody's views; that is reality, and, of course,
it is much more fantasy than the words. Supposing there had
been a film made of the life of our Lord. Do you think that that
would have stirred men as the Gospels have?

Q. *If I can reply one more time, if the Spirit of the Lord had
worked with it, yes. But I take your point about words being more
specific, and visuals more blunt. The use of visuals to inform people
of facts that they then believe are true because they have seen them,*

is a problem, but I do not believe it is an insuperable problem. Since you've spent three lectures directed basically against fantasy, as one of the most brilliant exponents of fantasy language, I find that I could talk a lot further with you on that. Today we had Nicodemus as a potential panel game expert; last week we had caterpillars guessing on radio whether they were going to be butterflies or not. The reason that we believe what you're saying, and take the message of what you're saying, is because we understand that you are using fantasy to enable us to see further. I think television can be used in that same way.

A. This is a matter of semantics. When I use the word 'fantasy', I do not mean the imagination, because the imagination is the heart and source of all art. Coleridge has a splendid exposition of the difference between fancy, or fantasy, and the imagination. When Blake said he believed in the imagination, he saw the imagination as providing an image of truth. But fantasy is the creation of images and ideas which are not truth, which have no relation to truth, and which cannot have a relation to truth. That is the point of Blake's observation about seeing with and through the eye. Seeing through the eye is this marvellous gift of imagination, which you are confusing with fantasy. It's an entirely different thing — like the difference between sentimentality and sentiment.

CHAIRMEN'S SPEECHES

CHAIRMAN'S SPEECH

BY SIR CHARLES CURRAN
DIRECTOR-GENERAL OF THE BBC
ON THE OCCASION OF THE FIRST LECTURE

I did warn John Stott, when he invited me to take the chair at the first of these lectures, that although it would give me great pleasure and be very entertaining to hear Malcolm Muggeridge on this occasion, I might find myself in some conflict with him, as I have in the past. I said that I've even been known to accuse him of Manichean pessimism in his attitude towards Christian belief and its social practice.

So Malcolm, having been duly warned, said he was prepared to take the risk if I *was* critical, and if he's talking about the media, then I know we take divergent views, because I value them, not uncritically, as they are, and I suspect that he is not nearly as convinced as I am about their present usefulness. When he adds that the title of his first lecture is 'The Fourth Temptation', I suspect that he really regards this as the work of the Devil.

So perhaps you'll forgive me if I recall at this point, some words which I spoke early in 1971 about what I see as the responsibilities of public broadcasters in this country. I said then: 'We do not understand by the phrase "moral responsibility" an obligation to preach a particular form of conduct.' I added that it was not our job to adopt a particular morality and then try to persuade everybody else to follow it. Because we in the BBC and other broadcasting organisations were monopolistic, or quasi-monopolistic, we could not be, *in the last resort*, a moral weapon, but only a means of conveying messages which may be moral according to the criteria which each of us in the audience applies. Finally, I suggested that during my time in the BBC I had seen the pluralistic society in which we now live reflected always among the membership of our board of governors, and having seen this, I could not believe that they would, I quote, 'ever have agreed on which morality should be espoused by the BBC'. For good measure I added: 'Nor do I know by what authority they would commit themselves to such a morality even if they were able collectively to agree on one.' I now add tonight: 'Nor do I know how any other broadcasting corporation outside a wholly theocratic state could reach any such agreement and commitment.'

And I must add finally, that as a Roman Catholic myself, I am only too conscious of being different from others and of the desire to be at one with other Christians. In that desire I see television as an indulgence, but not as a temptation. Now having thrown those few fire-crackers I leave it to Malcolm to light the blue touch-paper while I retire.

MALCOLM MUGGERIDGE

Ladies and gentlemen, I should like to begin by expressing my appreciation of Charles Curran's presence here this evening. It's a very friendly act on his part — especially as I gather it involves missing a Royal Command show at the Palladium — as well as a magnanimous one, because it is true that at different times over the years I've had hard things to say about the BBC over which he presides as heir to John Reith's kingdom, I think the fifth in succession. So that BBC bashing, at any rate by implication, may be considered derogatory to him. It is also true that by and large the BBC has treated me personally with consideration, if not indulgence. There was that fascinating, and so characteristic, directive once, to the effect that BBC documentaries must be impeccably objective except that James Cameron and I, presumably as balancing one another out, were permitted to air our fancies and prejudices.

Now, my occasional sallies at the Corporation's expense might therefore be regarded as exercises in biting the hand, but I'd like to see it differently. I've always thought myself that there was a very close resemblance between the BBC and the established Church of England. So that our chairman here this evening would be the primate, and the Chairmen of the Governors, Sir Michael Swann, would be the ecclesiastical commissioner, and the various departmental heads would be bishops, like there might be Alastair television and Edward radio and so on, all entitled to manifest their standing in the hierarchy by adding a tiny little microphone to their signatures. So, rather than as an ungrateful servant, I prefer to think of myself as some, at best, turbulent lay preacher, who is given to seizing any opportunity to be vociferous. Anyway, Charles, salutation, and don't forget that I have the dubious distinction of being probably the oldest, certainly the longest-standing practitioner on your books.

THE CHAIRMAN'S REPLY

I'm sure, Malcolm, that I should thank you on behalf of everybody for a marvellous oratorical feat. I have been conceded an immediate right of reply. I shall not take very long. After that, it will be my duty to pick out questioners from the floor. You will understand, after hearing Malcolm, the justice of the comment that my appearance here tonight is an act of magnanimity. I knew he thought we were the work of the Devil. However, be that as it may.

Let's go back to that motto for a moment, because it is a question of truth. It's in Latin, because one of the Governors thought he could write Latin. He was a Wykehamist, so he couldn't, and he cribbed a part of it from the Vulgate, which is not in the classical tradition of Latin. The truth is not always as it appears, even on the front of Broadcasting House.

But, out of the baroque elegance — and fantasy, of what Malcolm has said, we have to find an underlying structure of what he is trying to say. And I'm not sure that I can. He quoted, or rather deliberately misquoted, C. P. Scott, the famous 'Facts are sacred, comment should be free'. He didn't mention the second part of that quotation, 'It is good to be free. It is even better to be fair.'

It wasn't, on my watch, until seven o'clock that we came to the first mention of any programme which might justify the earlier strictures. And that mention was of a commercial in the United States, and a political commercial at that. And it wasn't actually about the commercial itself, it was about the making of the commercial. And five minutes later, we had the next mention of a programme, which was also about the making of the programme and not about the programme itself. I should not myself, as an arbiter of fairness within the BBC, regard that as something acceptable in one of our programmes.

The real salvo came at the beginning. 'Broadcasting is the greatest single influence on society at the moment.' I should be prepared to argue with that. I think there are other, very important influences. I would chose, I think, to remember in a fleeting moment, the family. However, let us dismiss the family, and let us accept that television is the greatest single influence. Exerted, and I have most of the exact words, arbitrarily, irresponsibly, without any spiritual conviction whatever. I simply say that this is not the world that I recognise myself as inhabiting when I live in broadcasting. All this, without one reference to any programme broadcast by the body which is guilty of this arbitrary and irresponsible action.

News. There was a long passage on news. Most of it was anecdotal, about the pre-television age, admittedly establishing

Malcolm's credentials as a media-man; not, I think, as a television man. There was a story about news from Cairo acquired by a non-Arabic-speaking journalist. It is possible for news to be collected in a better way. In April, I was in Madrid. I spent three hours with the present Prime Minister and his deputy, before they were the Prime Minister and deputy. I did speak Spanish, all the time. And I discovered, in that meeting, everything which has since happened. They told me exactly what was going to happen, and I will make a prophecy: they will do everything which is necessary to bring Spain into a constitutional democracy. That is what they told me; the evidence of what they have already done in fulfilment of what they said they would do is sufficient to convince me that what they were saying is true, and that true news has been reported. It is not always necessary for news to be untrue.

But the fundamental question was left unanswered. How *do* you run television? Do you run it by an assertion of your own assumptions, or those of others? Not in my world. Not under my faith, which rests on personal conviction and consent to what is proposed to be believed, and not by arbitrary imposition of what somebody says I must believe, regardless of whether I have understood it or accepted it. Somewhere along the way, in what Malcolm said, we lost Christ. Except for the history of the Church, and at that incomplete, no mention of the agonies and bitterness of the Reformation, and the four hundred years of difficulty which have gone on since. Just the splendours of the medieval church, which was sometimes not so splendid.

If television is going to be used by the churches, then it will have to be used for affirmation in the sense in which one of the Fathers described Christ's teaching: 'Love me, and do what you will.'

A. With respect, Sir Charles's closing quotation is misleading as he uses it. It is taken from Homily VII of St. Augustine's Homilies on St. John. The theme of the passage in question is as follows. There was a *traditio* (delivering up) of Jesus by God, the Father, by the Son, and by Judas. The thing done is the same, but the Father and the Son did it in love, whereas Judas did it in treacherous betrayal. If we measure the thing done by the divine intuition, in the case of the Father and the Son, it is to be admired, in the case of Judas to be condemned. Such is the force of charity (*agape*) that it alone distinguished the doings of men. 'Once for all then,' St. Augustine concludes, 'a short precept is given thee: LOVE, AND DO WHAT THOU WILT; whether thou hold thy peace, of love hold thy peace; whether thou cry out, of love cry out; whether thou correct, of love correct; whether thou spare, of love do thou spare: LET THE ROOT OF LOVE BE WITHIN, OF THIS ROOT CAN NOTHING SPRING BUT WHAT IS GOOD.'

CHAIRMAN'S SPEECH

BY SIR BRIAN YOUNG
DIRECTOR-GENERAL OF THE
INDEPENDENT BROADCASTING AUTHORITY
ON THE OCCASION OF THE SECOND LECTURE

Ladies and gentlemen, you will all remember what Hamlet said when on one occasion he encountered a head, very like Malcolm's: 'Alas, poor Yorick, a fellow of infinite jest.' Malcolm Muggeridge is, indeed, a 'fellow of infinite jest'. His wit and his prose style are, to my mind, quite unmatched. Add to these the charm, the vigorous flagellation of himself as well as others, and you can see why he is the most attractive monk of an unmonastic age.

My first encounter with him, a remote one, does make an ironic contrast with where we are this evening. Twenty years ago, as editor of *Punch*, he published something so shocking to that magazine's old public, that one of them, my father, cancelled his subscription. Like Malcolm now, he had his aerials taken out. And he wrote to this fellow Muggeridge to protest that in his passion to satisfy a rootless and immoral public, he was sweeping away all decent standards. My father told me what he'd done, for a headmaster should sympathise in matters of this kind. I asked to see the reply. I wish, I wish I could read it to you now, or indeed borrow phrases from it for the occasions when I now answer similar letters. But, alas, a silence followed. No reply.

Tonight it's all different. Malcolm fires the shafts, and I'm here to be St. Sebastian, together with Sir Michael Swann.

Malcolm began by telling us of the fourth temptation. But did a page drop out of his text? I believe that Christ in the temptations was working out how he should use his divine power to bring men to God. Not, he decided, through by-passing God's creative laws. He would not bribe men with material goods, dazzle them by riding the heavens, or coerce them as a magic king of the world. We know that he refused to turn stones into bread. But we know also that he did turn five loaves into food for thousands. And it seemed to me that the question that needed answering was whether Christ would let electronics multiply and hasten the spreading of his unique message in the same way that he multiplied and hastened the spreading of God's reign to be the food of many. Or would he think that distortion would be bound to turn his bread into stones? I heard no attempt to tackle the question. I heard only the surrounding jests.

But tonight, with the Dead Sea Videotapes, we shall fare better. For Malcolm Muggeridge is surely our twentieth-century Aristophanes. At a time when Athens reached a peak of civilisation, when every single citizen could sit with the decision-makers and every single citizen could go to the same play, quite a parallel there to broadcasting, all that Aristophanes could see was falling standards, gullible fools, grotesque demagogues. He mocked them with wit and fantasy, but in the middle of it, in the middle of the outrageous and distorting and delightful attacks, there was love, not merely love of the stable past, but love of his fellow men. And there are many shafts of perception among the brilliant horseplay. As Malcolm mocks and satirises the broadcasters tonight, I shall be looking in the text of his scrolls for what I find in the comedy of Aristophanes: insight as well as witty exaggeration, care as well as biting caricature.

* * *

Malcolm, thank you. That was eloquent and moving, and I claim no right of reply: I would merely occupy three minutes while some of you are thinking what you want to ask Malcolm, what you want to say to him. I thought now and then that he was wearing the opposite of rose-coloured spectacles. What are they, puce-coloured spectacles? I thought he was looking at the world and seeing only some very sad aspects of it, and I hope that some here, perhaps particularly the younger ones, will tell him some of the things which in his diagnosis he seems to me to miss. His words about the Incarnation, and about being thankful for it, reminded one of the need not to escape to the pure spirit, where in many ways he wanted to be, but to see in and through material things something of God's goodness.

He obviously has very strong feelings indeed about images. Iconoclasts, I think they were, the last people who insisted that all images should be broken. I think Malcolm's feeling was, so to speak, an upside-down Narcissus: he'd looked at an image of himself, and instead of loving it had felt a hatred for it because he knew so much about what seemed to him the falsity, the artificial means by which that image was brought to the screen. I'm not sure that that is a very profound cause for rejecting images, and it seems to me that many of the parables are images, and if I could throw in one thought it would be of an image — the third chapter of Genesis, one of the most powerful images ever. Maybe broadcasting is rather like the tree of the knowledge of good and evil, that image of every man growing up from innocence to the point of choice and freedom, maybe of the whole of mankind growing into that: the taking of the fruit symbolises the more difficult choosing, living dangerously. But remember the second image — somewhere in the Fathers, I think — where that same tree is taken, and is set up on Calvary to be the upright of a cross; and putting forth the old roots once more in the ground, it does flower again.

I believe that the fruits for which we are responsible, in a very vivid and visible form, as Malcolm has reminded us — we broadcasters bring them to people in a way which provokes much controversy — I believe that these fruits (some of them, of course, are not particularly nourishing, they are there for an evening's relaxation; some of them, certainly, do have the show-biz elements which Malcolm and others dislike) — I do believe that more of them than he allowed bring a sense of compassion and concern, and wonder, and admiration, in fiction as well as non-fiction, despite his quotation from Simone Weil; and so perhaps, in discussion, we could pursue not only those elements in the modern world seen particularly in the media which may invoke our dislike, but also those elements which give us hope and courage too. Now that must have given you time enough to think of questions, comments and ways to carry on the debate.

CHAIRMAN'S SPEECH

BY THE REVEREND JOHN R. W. STOTT
CHAIRMAN ON THE OCCASION
OF THE FINAL LECTURE

I would like to take just a few minutes if I may to express our united gratitude to Malcolm Muggeridge. If I may say so, I'm extremely hesitant to do so, partly because I fear that I may well be one of those trendy and long-haired clergymen that Malcolm Muggeridge loses no opportunity to anathematise. Nevertheless, I do want to say two things, one about him and the second about ourselves.

Some of you may know that Malcolm Muggeridge has returned only just before the lectures began, from what I can only describe as a triumphal procession in Australia and New Zealand. Dr. Marcus Loane, the Archbishop of Sydney, described him in a meeting of the Synod in Sydney as 'the most significant layman since C. S. Lewis, highly intelligent and an outstandingly articulate apologist for Christ'. A friend of mine wrote to me just after Malcolm Muggeridge's visit to Sydney to say that he made a real impact on pagan Australia, as well as on Christian Australia, and then added, I think significantly, 'Oh, for more prophets, dear Lord!'

Now I would like to suggest to you that we should regard Malcolm Muggeridge as a true prophet of the twentieth century, and I take the liberty for just a moment of characterising for you the Prophet Muggeridge. This is how I want to express my gratitude, and I hope yours, for him.

First he has courage. While Christian civilisation seems to be crumbling around us in the West, and there is an urgent need for Christian leadership, Malcolm Muggeridge again and again is a voice crying in the wilderness.

Next, he has perception. The prophets were seers, they saw issues with limpid clarity while others remained in the gathering gloom. Have you noticed how often in the past lectures Malcolm Muggeridge has said, and not least in the question time, 'This is how I see it'. He often sees things that we don't see, sees things in Blake's phrase that he's been using tonight, 'through and not just with the eyes'.

Next, prophets are awkward fellows to live with. They denounce evil, they sound an alarm, while the nation is peacefully sleeping; while they have at the same time deep compassion for the nation and the culture which they are criticising.

And, sometimes, prophets exaggerate. Strict, mathematical accuracy is not their strong point. Now as I've listened to Malcolm Muggeridge's three lectures I've found myself casting him in the joint rôle of Elijah and John the Baptist, because they are equivalents in the two Testaments. I don't find it hard or difficult to visualise Malcolm in the ascetic garb of camel's hair and loin cloth. I don't find it difficult to imagine him munching locusts with relish, or even crying, 'I, even I only, am left'. But you know, the interesting thing is that the Lord God had to make, or help Elijah make, drastic adjustment of his figures. Elijah had dropped a clanger: he was out by seven thousand. But the point that I want to make is that God did not jettison Elijah on that account. I sum it up like this: I believe that in the reckoning of God, prophetic faithfulness is more important than strict statistical accuracy.

I've a final thing to say now. That's my way, Malcolm, of thanking you: I hope very much that you don't mind the loin cloth and the rest, and the locusts. The final word, and it's only very brief, is about ourselves.

Christians all down the ages have been debating with one another as to what our attitude to the world should be, whether we deny it, renounce it, affirm it, transform it, change it, etc. etc., and all that has been on our minds during these lectures. For myself, I want to appeal to you as chairman, to those of you who belong to the rising generation of Christians, that you will get into the media and salt them. I myself believe, you see, the media go wrong, and the BBC and all that — it's no good blaming them: when the meat goes bad it's no good blaming the meat and the bacteria that are making the meat putrefy: it's the fault of the salt that's not there to stop it from going bad. And if the media have gone bad, so bad that we want to take our aerials out, who is to blame? Are you pointing the finger at them? Over there? I point the finger here. It's *our* fault. It's the fault of Christian people. If only we could be the salt of the earth as we were meant to be, and refine, and reform and rescue for Jesus Christ. But as we seek to do so, do let us keep hearing the alarm bell that Malcolm has been so faithfully ringing and so loudly in these lectures. I shall for myself never in all my life forget the contrast that he's been drawing between fantasy and reality, and I hope the thing I'm going to take with me is his words in the lecture last week: stay with the reality of Christ. Lash yourself to the reality of Christ, like sailors in a stormy sea. I leave these lectures with a fresh determination to do even that in this fantasy world in which we live. So Malcolm, we thank you very much indeed, and even more we thank Jesus Christ, whose reality shines, if we may say so, very brightly in yourself. Thank you.

MEDIA BOOKS

Understanding Media: The Extension of Man and *The Gutenberg Galaxy*, by Marshall McLuhan — may be regarded as classics on the subject despite proneness to wild and sometimes crazy generalities. This tendency is carried further in *The Medium is the Massage*, though here, too, some excellent points are made — e.g. 'You must talk to the media not to the programmer. To talk to the programmer is like complaining to a hot-dog vendor at a ballpark about how badly your favourite team is playing.' For a critique by a sometime disciple, see Jonathan Miller's *McLuhan*, which does an effective demolition job, though in manner at times out-McLuhanising McLuhan.

The Gods of the Antenna by Bruce Herschensohn — a carefully documented, blow-by-blow account of how, through the machinations of the media, the United States lost a war and a President — perhaps the Presidency, too.

News From Nowhere by Edward Jay Epstein — a conscientious study of the concoction and presentation of TV news on behalf of one of the large American networks. A great deal of relevant data is assembled — for instance, this from a former Saigon bureau chief: '*It is considered standard operating procedure for troops to fire their weapons for the benefit of cameramen. If our cameramen had to wait until a fire fight with the Vietkong broke out, we'd have much less footage — and perhaps cameramen.*'

Facing the Nation, Television and Politics 1936-76, by Grace Wyndham Goldie, affectionately designated as a woman of iron whim in the days of her benign but inflexible rule over BBC Talks and Current Affairs. Those who knew her, worked with her and loved her, will wish that she had injected more of the rare and wonderful piquancy of her character and style of utterance into her account of her stewardship. Even so, she describes with unique authority the fluctuating relations between government and media as they developed from the very beginning of television to the present day.

The Ravenous Eye by Milton Shulman — a sometime TV producer and TV critic casts a sceptical and critical eye over the output of the networks, with special reference to a 'fifth factor' — the effect on the young of constant exposure to scenes of violence and depravity.

Television: the Ephemeral Art by T. C. Worsley — a sensitive, perceptive analysis of the craft and craftiness of television practitioners, by another television critic, one of the best, now, alas, dead.

About Television by Martin Mayer — the author sees television for what it is; not as a new art form or a window on the world, but as a projection of tabloid journalism with special potentialities and dangers of its own. His attitude is well illustrated by a remark quoted from a commentary on a New York season of 'good' TV — '*Sub specie aeternitatis*, everything was lousy'. A blood-curdling shape of things to come is envisaged, in which every home is built round an entertainment centre with up to a hundred channels feeding into it offering an immense choice of programmes, and a cable system hooked into a computerised videotape library making available hundreds of thousands of programmes. Good Lord, deliver us!

Richard Dimbleby, by Jonathan Dimbleby — a son's filial but discerning biography of the one-and-only Media Panjandrum of our time — *après lui le déluge*.

Day by Day — Robin Day on Robin Day, tellyman.

The Shadow in the Cave by Anthony Smith — referred to in Lecture Three, page 73.

Due to Circumstances Beyond Our Control . . . by Fred Friendly, who was for some sixteen years a dominating figure in the CBS network, when he worked closely with Ed Murrow. His favourite dictum — 'Because television can make so much money doing its worst, it often cannot afford to do its best' — is his text in this interesting and valuable collection of media reminiscences.

OTHER USEFUL BOOKS:
The Hungry Eye, an inside look at TV by Eugene Paul.

The New Priesthood, a series of interviews with people concerned in the production of television by Joan Bakewell and Nicholas Garnham.

Tomorrow's Television, an examination of British broadcasting, past, present and future by Andrew Quicke.

THEN REPORTS:
Violence On Television, a BBC Audience Research Department Report, *Fram*, a Report on the Oslo Assembly of the World Association for Christian Communication, and *Broadcasting, Society and the Church*, a Report of the Broadcasting Commission of the General Synod of the Church of England — just three of the innumerable reports on broadcasting in which the incidence of expressions like 'areas of concern' and 'meaningful dialogue' and of sentences like 'the themes of these most popular messages seem to make up a composite reciprocal of the values stressed in adult socialisation' are well up to average.